PRAISE FOR
WHERE DO BROKEN HEARTS GO?
HEALING AND HOPE AFTER ABORTION:

"Jane Abbate's *Where Do Broken Hearts Go?* is truly an extraordinary gift to those who read it. It is a masterful guide that will help heal loneliness and guilt. If you have had an abortion, I strongly urge you to read this life-changing book and experience the freedom in receiving God's forgiving love."

—Dale Hayden, MA Marital Therapist, Relationships That Heal

"Whether you have had one or more abortions, Jane hits the issues right on the head with care and compassion. I wish I had this book sooner to help me with my own healing."

—Pamela Drazinski

"*Where Do Broken Hearts Go?* is an inspiring account of one woman's ongoing journey toward healing. This book can help both men and women to understand and move beyond their grief and find a renewed hope for their lives."

—Jason Baier, Founder, Fatherhood Forever Foundation

www.fatherhoodforever.org

"I am thrilled to see a book that is so open and honest about abortion and especially appreciate the genuine compassion, warmth and caring that Jane Abbate shows on every page of this book. You will find answers to questions and healing within your heart as she walks you gently into the arms of the Savior and into new found liberty!"

—Kathryn Bonner, Author of *Confessions of a Pastor's Wife*, Speaker, Life Purpose Coach, Radio Host and founder of www.kathrynbonnerministries.com

"*Where Do Broken Hearts Go?* is a profound and deeply moving book. Jane Abbate's compelling testimony, teaching, and reflection exercises will capture your attention from beginning to end.

You will gain new insights and be moved to compassion as you read her story of healing and restoration. This soul-stirring book offers women everywhere a chance to be transformed and restored by the Father's love as they move forward in His divine design for their lives."

—Marykay Moore, Pastor and Life Purpose Coach

"*Where Do Broken Hearts Go?* is a wonderful resource for those who assist in the abortion recovery process. While women and men grieve differently, they both must work through the stages that Jane Abbate has outlined in this book. The reflection exercises are meaningful, purposeful and directed. This book is a beneficial addition to the library of abortion recovery materials that therapists use with clients seeking to find healing from past abortion(s)."

—Abigayle A. Koller, MA, MSW, LSW
Abortion Recovery Therapist

WHERE DO BROKEN HEARTS GO?

HEALING AND HOPE AFTER ABORTION

WHERE DO BROKEN HEARTS GO?

HEALING AND
HOPE AFTER
ABORTION

JANE ABBATE

Messy
Miracles
Books

Where Do Broken Hearts Go?
Copyright © 2010 Jane Abbate
Published by Messy Miracles, PO Box 22, Wildwood, PA 15091-1001

Disclaimer: This book is intended for general education purposes only. It is not intended as a substitute for therapy, as a "self-help" guide, or as a training manual for therapists interested in post-abortion counseling. If expert assistance or counseling is needed, the services of a competent professional should be sought.

First Edition
Publisher's Cataloging-In-Publication
Abbate, Jane.
    Where do broken hearts go? : healing and hope after abortion / Jane
    Abbate. -- 1st ed. -- Pittsburgh, PA : Messy Miracles Books, c2010.
        p. ; cm.
        ISBN-13: 978-0-9828486-0-9
    Includes bibliographical references.
        1. Abortion--Psychological aspects. 2. Post-abortion syndrome.
    3. Abortion--Religious aspects--Christianity. 4. Abortion counseling.
    I. Title.
    HQ767.4 .A33 2010
    363.46--dc22   1009

Printed in the United States of America on acid-free paper.
Editor: Pamela Guerrieri, www.proofedtoperfection.com
Cover and Book Design: Patricia Bacall, www.bacallcreative.com
Cover Copy: Laren Bright, www.larenbright.com

Attention Non-Profit Organizations, Churches, Colleges, Universities, and Professional Organizations: Quantity discounts are available on bulk purchases of this book for educational training, fund raising, or gift-giving. For more information contact Messy Miracles, PO Box 22, Wildwood, PA 15091.

CONTENTS

To my husband, Bill, a true man of God.
Words cannot express my appreciation, love and honor for you.
I am most richly blessed.

PREFACE

In my private counseling practice of over thirty years, two of the constant issues of concern for my clients are guilt and shame. There are few psychological struggles as crippling as these. And in many instances, those emotional issues are a direct result of abortion, for both men and women.

The effects of abortion are devastating. One's emotional, psychological and spiritual sides are dramatically impacted; at times, even the physical side. As a consequence, one's whole identity of self is negatively affected. Many times clients who have had one or more abortions share with me that they believe they do not deserve to be loved, accepted, or forgiven. They believe they deserve to be punished and rejected. As a result, the weight of this particular shame and guilt drives abortion survivors into isolation and deep despair.

However, God has not left us without hope. One of the most wonderful and liberating aspects of the Gospel is the forgiveness and acceptance found in a personal relationship with Jesus Christ. Ultimately, in him we have all we need to find the meaning, fullness, and purpose of our lives, and the freedom from disabling guilt and shame.

In this book, Jane Abbate presents in a very understandable and self-directed manner how one can experience healing from the effects of abortion. She writes with genuine transparency and compassion that allows each person to explore this path in a personal way.

In a workbook format, Ms. Abbate presents a practical self-study guide, in thought-provoking sections, a way to better understand the psychological effects of abortion and how to discover the healing and wholeness found in Christ's love. This book is helpful, not just for individuals, but for pastors, therapists, psychologists, counselors or anyone in the helping profession. The format allows for both individual and small group study.

This book is a must read for those wishing to experience God's love and forgiveness in dealing with abortion. It will be well worth the journey. I encourage you to take the risk.

Scott E. Barber, Ph.D.

Psychologist

Wexford, PA

In Appreciation For:

Tara, Martha, Joan, Bridget and Betsy: You were the first to hear my story and you received it with kindness and compassion. God bless you, wherever you are.

Ann Depner: Thank you for bringing RV to Pittsburgh and for being my role model, collaborator and encourager.

Scott Barber, Dale Hayden, Tawnya Knierim, Karen LaFrance and Jan Wein: Because of your wisdom and willingness to share your experience, this book has greater depth and insight.

Katie and Pamela: I am proud to call you my sisters from the Vineyard. Thank you for reviewing the book and adding so much more to it.

Melodie Leake: Your spiritual guidance and wisdom kept me grounded and focused in the right direction.

Pamela Guerrieri: It was a privilege to work with you as my editor. You far exceeded my expectations and I could not have done this without you.

Mike Craven, Adele Lynn, Kally Reynolds, Maria Berdusco and Brenda Vester: Sharing your experience with publishing was a great help.

Patricia Bacall: You are an awesome designer. Thank you for your flexibility and patience.

Terri McKay: You are the most creative person I know. Thank you for your friendship and help—one more time!

Mary Ellen, Ann Leslie and Sally: Now you know the whole story and you love me still. You are amazing and I love you dearly.

INTRODUCTION

Abortion—the word may prompt chills of horror for some and a memory hard to forget for others. Many find it to be no big deal, simply a difficult recollection of a seemingly necessary choice. Yet, no matter where you come from or what your past holds, abortion is a heated topic of debate and tough subject to talk about. Bring it up and moral judgments and political agendas get triggered. But for millions of women who know abortion firsthand, it is a deeply emotional and complex experience. It is a life-changing experience.

Many people are surprised to learn that abortion is one of the most common surgical procedures performed in the United States with over one million pregnancies terminated each year[1]. Women under the age of 25 account for half of all abortions, and three-fourths of all abortions occur to women under age 30. Believe it or not, at current rates, research estimates that one out of every three women will have at least one abortion by age 45[2].

Sadly, these are not merely shocking statistics about what happens to other people out there; they reveal the story of *my* life, and they may reflect your own life as well. *Where Do Broken Hearts Go?* shares the aftermath of my encounter with three abortions. Unwed, frightened, and ashamed, each time I faced an unplanned pregnancy I felt unprepared to care for a child. Like many women, I thought abortion would solve a dilemma. I did not anticipate the problems it would cause or understand how it would impact the rest of my life.

Abortion is a trauma that wreaked havoc on my emotional and spiritual well-being. Initially, and for many years to follow, I grew numb, protecting myself from uncomfortable and shameful feelings that plagued me.

Unfortunately, time does not heal all wounds! It just allowed my hurts to fester and, in the meantime, my entire life became infected and damaged by emotions I could not interpret or did not know what to do with. As one of millions of women who experienced the trauma of repeat abortions, the emotional pain was particularly confusing and complicated. While there are some who do not believe in such a thing as postabortion stress, I know that the emotional anguish of my abortions was real. Denying and avoiding my feelings interfered with my ability to experience a full life and caused me to push away and hurt those I cared about.

Twenty years after my last abortion, something I could not explain compelled me to want to comprehend, resolve, and find meaning in what happened. While it has not been easy to explore this absolute worst part of my life, I thank God for the courage to accept the gravity of what I have done and the humility to accept his forgiveness. His reward for my faithfulness was allowing me to discover my capacity to love, to feel joy, and to find hope again.

How To Read This Book

Where Do Broken Hearts Go? focuses on and explains the emotions that dominated my life after my abortions. Are these the only emotional responses that result from abortion? No. Will everyone feel the same way in the same sequence and with the same intensity? No. Are my abortions the only triggers that cause me to have these feelings? No. Is it possible to gain relief from thorny feelings and enjoy positive emotions more frequently? *Yes!*

There is no neat path to healing and wholeness when dealing with the after effects of abortion. Just as the circumstances that led to your abortion were different from mine, so will our experiences afterward vary. Some emotions may hit you at the same time, much later, or not at all. You may experience them in any order, and for some people there is often much looping back until the root issues are resolved.

Because many of us tell very few trusted friends, or no one, about our abortions, we are left to deal with the emotional aftermath on our own. Outsiders may not understand the distress you are going through, even for years afterward, and might question, "What's the matter with you?" Just know that your need to understand and process each tender or painful emotion is normal.

Emotions are a gift from God. It is not sinful or inappropriate to express them. They are sources of information about what we are thinking and what drives our behavior. It wasn't until I had processed such troubling emotions as anger, regret, and loneliness that more positive feelings of gratitude, peace, and freedom emerged. Keep in mind that there is no right way to grieve or process your own experience. So, while some may find it helpful to read the chapters of the book in sequence, others may choose to skip around, finding a chapter that speaks to them in their current frame of mind.

I encourage you to take the time to complete the Reflection Exercises included at the end of each chapter. These sections are designed as a guide to exploring your emotions on a deeper level so that you may come to greater self-understanding. To get the most out of the reflecting process, you may choose to write down your thoughts in the pages provided in each section and at the back of the book. You might also choose to keep a separate notebook handy to record your responses in detail, to capture further insights, or to jot down a prayer that comes to mind. Journaling is often an effective way to bring thoughts to the surface and can be referenced later when you need it.

Each chapter concludes with a Bible verse chosen specifically to instruct, console, or inspire you. These Scriptures are God's words to you, and they are evidence of his unfailing love and faithfulness, no matter what you have done. I encourage you to read each verse aloud and then pour your heart out to God by reading the suggested prayer that follows or say a prayer of your own. Either way, communicate with the One who loves you unconditionally, for his ears are always open.

While this book presents a general guide for women who have had abortions, it is not a substitute for professional therapy or sound spiritual direction. In fact, I took advantage of both to help me confront and move on from my past. Men who have experienced abortion may also relate to my emotional and spiritual struggles because they are also deeply wounded by the loss of their children. In these cases the Reflection Exercises, Bible verses, and prayers can be effective tools of healing for men as well.

Regardless of whether you are a woman or a man reading this book, I urge you to pursue all available resources and take steps toward a rich and satisfying life. That is what God wants for you: *"I came so they can have real and eternal life, more and better life than they ever dreamed of"* (John 10:10, MSG).

More Than an Emotional Battle

Common misconceptions in today's society support abortion as a perfectly acceptable alternative because it is a legal medical procedure. Others take the opposing view that those who make the choice do not deserve to be forgiven. No matter what the trend is, I am convinced that abortion is a serious sin and that many of us need to stop denying or justifying our actions. It is time to repair the damage to our physical and emotional well-being, as well as to our relationships with others. But we should not overlook the spiritual wound that also needs to be healed. Personal guilt and shame, coupled with the horrified and condemning reactions of others, can lead us to believe we have committed an unforgivable sin. At the time when we need God the most, we may actually cut off or distance ourselves from him.

Make no mistake. Healing from abortion is not just an emotional battle; you are fighting for your soul. But you are not the enemy. There is one, however, who will do anything and everything in his power to keep you doubting God's love and mercy. This enemy wants to control your thoughts, your beliefs, your emotions—everything you say and do—so that he can control where you spend eternity. I sincerely believe that our greatest enemy is very real and that his name is Satan.

I realize that some people may be put off by the mention of the Evil One, but please do not allow yourself to be fooled. If you are tempted to put this book down, know that this is a sure sign that Satan has been stirred up and is threatened by your reading this. His goal for your life is to steal your peace and joy and separate you from God. One of his prime strategies is to keep you churning in self-condemnation, imprisoned by confusion and grief. Satan is a master manipulator, an aggressive enemy who craftily uses others to confuse you by telling you to move on and stop thinking about your abortion, or that there is nothing wrong with abortion in the first place. But you must be just as aggressive about resisting these lies!

Staying spiritually strong is your greatest weapon against your greatest enemy. You cannot stop the enemy from putting destructive thoughts into your mind, but you do not have to dwell on them. As you read this book and explore your abortion experience in more depth, if you find yourself gripped by a difficult emotion, immediately turn to the Bible verse in that chapter and read it aloud or simply say, "Jesus, help me!" Just whispering Jesus' name offers powerful protection against the one who most wants to keep you in the dark.

One final note of encouragement: Life is about moving through, moving on, growing up, and growing through each and every experience. God will bless you for your courage and comfort you for your faithfulness as you examine your life—especially your experience of abortion. I know this is true because he said it in Isaiah 40:1–2 (MSG): *"Comfort, oh comfort my people," says your God. "Speak softly and tenderly to Jerusalem, but also make it very clear that she has served her sentence that her sin is taken care of—forgiven! She's been punished enough and more than enough, and now it's over and done with."*

Chapter 1

Numbness

Definition: incapable of action or of feeling emotion

Hold on a minute! This book is supposed to be about how to deal with the wide range of emotions that a woman might experience following an abortion. How could the first chapter be about feeling nothing at all?

Actually, numbness is not a sign that a woman is void of feelings about what has happened to her; rather, it reflects *overwhelming* emotion—to the point where it becomes more than she is capable of dealing with at the time. Coping with the impact of abortion can be complicated by the circumstances leading up to the decision, the trauma of the procedure itself, and the reactions—real or expected—of people afterward. No matter why or how it occurs, abortion is a stressful experience, often shrouded in secrecy and shame.

The story of my abortions is not easy to share. First of all, there is very little that I remember about the time before, during, and after the procedures. I can pull together bits and pieces, but long periods of time are missing from memory. I struggle to explain how I could find myself unmarried and pregnant *three times*. It is also amazing to me that each time I simply moved on, as if nothing had happened. If abortion is so hurtful, why did it take me so long to recognize and deal with it?

While each scenario was unique, the pain burrowing into my soul grew more and more familiar. I underwent my first abortion when I was twenty-two years old; the father was my college boyfriend. I became pregnant the second time at age twenty-six to a young man I met at a disco and dated briefly. The third abortion occurred when I was thirty-two and the father was a married man. Two abortions occurred in abortion clinics, one in a hospital. I was alone for each one. The fathers of my first two children never knew about the pregnancies. The third man knew and wholeheartedly supported my decision to abort our child.

Each time I discovered I was pregnant, I was overwhelmed with panic and dread. I feared what my family and friends would think of me. And the third pregnancy would surely expose my secret, adulterous affair. The thought of childbirth was petrifying and I felt unprepared to be a mother. Each fear suffocated me more and more, and by the time each abortion was over, the stress had deadened me to the reality of what I had done. I was relieved that my immediate problem was over. Then I became numb.

This is typical. Many women report feeling immediately "relieved" that their "problem is solved" following an abortion. Research by the Elliot Institute showed that over 60 percent of women surveyed reported that there was a period of time when they would not have reported any negative feelings about their abortion[3].

Abortion affects people in different ways. Memories of this traumatic event can be either intensely clear or completely repressed. Some women remember vivid details of the procedure, unable to push the haunting thoughts out of mind. One study showed that many women report flashbacks triggered by certain sights, sounds, or smells that recall specific details of their abortion[4]. Dreams, nightmares, and sleep disorders are common problems among women with abortion in their past. With the conscious mind sleeping, defense mechanisms are relaxed and distressing memories and emotions can emerge in both explicit and symbolic dreams.

Others share my experience, remembering very little. Reality can be so distressing that we emotionally exit the scene and deaden ourselves to what is happening. Many women describe feeling disoriented during the procedure itself, getting through it by distancing themselves from the event as though it were happening to someone else. This type of emotional amnesia, which can be total or partial, temporary or permanent, is common among women enduring a traumatic reaction to abortion.

Unfortunately, one painful memory I do have of my last abortion is sitting in a Chinese restaurant with the baby's father after the procedure, making plans for the weekend. A friend who also experienced three abortions shared a recollection of going to the movies afterward with her husband, neither one of them ever again mentioning what happened. Delayed reactions can take five or more years to manifest, during which time post-abortive women seem to simply pick up their lives and move on. Some might interpret this "unfeeling" behavior as cold, heartless, and uncaring. That is far from the truth. The fact is, we were in shock and unable to deal with the truth of what we had just been through.

In the meantime, we live behind walls of denial, numb to our emotions, protecting ourselves from the aftermath of our decision. Living in this empty shell of existence allows us to simply cope but not truly live. Only by confronting the past and dealing with it can we become whole again, no longer anesthetized to our feelings.

The path to healing requires us to recognize the symptoms of our distress and break down our defenses. Painful though it will be, I promise you that becoming clear about your abortion past will free you to create a better and more satisfying future. Healing from abortion takes time, and I believe it continues for the rest of our lives. Be patient and gentle with yourself. That is what your Father in heaven wants you to do.

REFLECTION EXERCISE

Abortion: How Does it Affect You?

Distress over your abortion may have occurred within a few hours following your abortion, or it may not have surfaced until many years later. You may be afraid to talk about it, or perhaps you are overcome with great shame or do not even realize how your decision affects you. The following questions can help you better understand how abortion has impacted your life and lead you to recover from your loss:

1. Do you find yourself struggling to turn off feelings connected to your abortion, perhaps telling yourself repeatedly to forget about it and just get on with your life?

   Yes____ No____

2. Are you negatively affected by books, magazines, and television programs that deal with the subject of babies, pregnant women, or abortion?

   Yes____ No____

3. Are you uncomfortable around pregnant women or children?

   Yes____ No____

4. Do you get nervous or avoid doctors, doctor's offices, hospitals, or things medically-related?

   Yes____ No____

5. Are there certain times of the year you find yourself depressed, sick, or accident-prone, especially around the anniversary date of the abortion or the due date of the baby?

   Yes____ No____

6. Are you resentful and unforgiving toward anyone because of his or her involvement (or lack of involvement!) in your abortion—such as a boyfriend, husband, parents, other friends, or the medical personnel who performed your abortion?

Yes___ No___

7. Are you putting yourself in a situation where you could find yourself faced with another unwanted pregnancy?

Yes___ No___

8. Do you have trouble with emotional intimacy or relationships since your abortion?

Yes___ No___

9. Do you avoid sex or do you have trouble with physical affection or intimacy?

Yes___ No___

10. Are you practicing irresponsible sexual behavior now, perhaps showing indifference regarding who you have sex with?

Yes___ No___

11. Are you still in a relationship with the partner you had the abortion with, and unwilling to end it because then it would feel like the abortion was "for nothing"?

Yes___ No___

12. Did you marry, or rush into marriage with, the man who made you pregnant in order to "justify" having the abortion?

Yes___ No___

13. Are you obsessed with excelling at work or school, expecting yourself and other people to be perfect?

Yes___ No___

14. Have you experienced periods of prolonged depression since your abortion? Have you had any suicidal thoughts or attempts?

Yes___ No___

15. Have you experienced a numbing of emotions, unable to feel strongly about anything?

Yes____ No____

16. Has any drug or alcohol use occurred or become more frequent since the abortion? Have you started or increased any self-harming behaviors (cutting, anorexia/bulimia, etc.)?

Yes____ No____

17. Do you have sleeping problems (difficulty falling asleep, difficulty staying asleep, or wanting to sleep too much)?

Yes____ No____

18. Do you have trouble with anxiety and/or panic attacks?

Yes____ No____

19. Are you able to talk about your abortion?

Yes____ No____

20. Do you sometimes feel guilty or remorseful about your abortion? Do you grieve for the loss of your baby?

Yes____ No____

21. Do you fear you will never be able to have children/more children?

Yes____ No ____

22. If you have children now, do you smother them with your love or over-protect them? Do you worry excessively about them getting hurt?

Yes____ No____

23. If you have children now, do you have problems mothering them, feel distant from them, or feel "unable to bond" with them?

Yes____ No____

24. Do you have concerns about your ability to be a good mother?

Yes____ No____

25. Do you get a "funny feeling" in your stomach at the thought of discussing/debating pro-life or pro-choice issues? Do you purposely avoid any discussion or information involving these issues?

Yes___ No___

26. Has your self-esteem changed since your abortion?

Yes___ No___

27. Did your relationship with God or your spirituality change after your abortion?

Yes___ No___

Information about Post Abortion Stress Syndrome

If you have answered "yes" to several of the above questions, and especially if you felt angry about or upset by any of the questions, or had an emotional or physical response to any of them, you may be suffering from a problem known as Post Abortion Stress Syndrome (PASS). There is evidence that some women experience emotional aftermath that can deeply disturb their lives.

Support groups, such as Rachel's Vineyard Ministries, and Bible studies, such as Forgiven and Set Free, are available to help you understand and recover from the emotional aftermath of abortion. Professional counseling with someone who is familiar with PASS can also be helpful and, when combined with spiritual direction or pastoral counseling, can lead to physical, emotional, and spiritual healing.

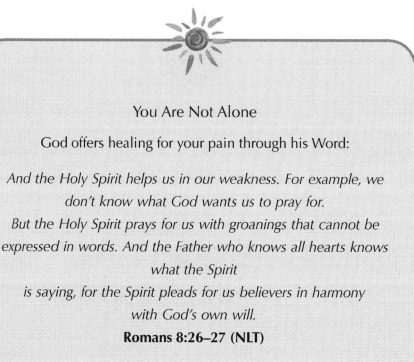

You Are Not Alone

God offers healing for your pain through his Word:

*And the Holy Spirit helps us in our weakness. For example, we
don't know what God wants us to pray for.*
*But the Holy Spirit prays for us with groanings that cannot be
expressed in words. And the Father who knows all hearts knows
what the Spirit*
*is saying, for the Spirit pleads for us believers in harmony
with God's own will.*
Romans 8:26–27 (NLT)

Pray:

Dear God, your Holy Spirit is said to help those who do not know
how to pray and I am not sure where or how to begin. What has
happened to me is overwhelming and I do not want to face it. The
shame and grief that I feel are so painful that sometimes I would
rather feel nothing at all. But I know that it is time to stop avoiding
my feelings. Even though I do not know the right words to say and I
do not feel worthy to ask for your help, please give me the strength
to pray right now and every day ahead in the days to come. I trust
that you will always do what is best for me. Amen.

NOTES

NOTES

_____

_____

_____

_____

_____

_____

_____

_____

_____

_____

_____

_____

_____

_____

_____

_____

_____

_____

_____

_____

_____

_____

Chapter 2

Heartbreak

Definition: overwhelming sorrow, grief, or disappointment

At twenty-two years old, life was good! I was excited about starting my career and had landed a good job as a management trainee. Soon I would be able to afford my own apartment and really be out on my own. I was loving life! One of my favorite things to do in my free time was cycling, and there was a local park where my friends and I often rode on Saturday afternoons. One day, in the summer of 1977, I unsuccessfully attempted to jump a curb with my ten-speed bicycle. Flying over the handlebars, I slid twenty feet across asphalt pavement, coming to a stop when my head hit the guardrail. Severe road rash on my knees and hands made my injuries obvious for everyone to see.

In the days that followed, friends and family reached out to help, their flowers and cards a welcomed source of comfort. Thanks to good first aid, my cuts healed quickly and eventually the bruises faded. A helmet saved me from a concussion. I was back to work and bike riding again in several weeks, a few nasty-looking scars being the only signs of the trauma I had experienced.

Just a few months later, I found myself experiencing a much more difficult trauma, although I didn't recognize it as one at the time. Pregnant and unmarried, I was stunned by the prospect of having a baby. Ashamed and intimidated by what my parents might say and what others would think, I was petrified to talk to anyone. It seemed there was only one option. In panic, I chose to have an abortion.

Unlike the unmistakable injuries from my bicycle accident, the emotional and spiritual wounds caused by my abortion were well hidden. Like many women, I simply picked up the next day where I had left off, acting as if everything was perfectly normal. But eventually the emotional wounds appeared. My career began to consume me and a pattern took hold. Driven to succeed, I was always on the lookout so I could get ahead and do even better. When the recognition or promotion I was sure I deserved did not happen, I blamed myself and was tormented by feelings of inadequacy. The more money I made, the more I desired even better clothes, jewelry, and expensive cars. By the time I reached my thirties, I was feeling emotionally exhausted and defeated.

Meanwhile, my personal life was a disaster. I became increasingly promiscuous, meeting many sexual partners in the discos and bars where I spent most Friday and Saturday nights. While I had several girlfriends who enjoyed the club life too, over time, I neglected relationships with childhood and college friends. I think, on some level, I turned away from those who would be most likely to comfort and support me, believing they would not be able to handle my shameful secret.

All the while I was building a persona of success, self-confidence, and independence, I would not allow myself to think about the fact that I had lost *my baby*. Some might say I was heartless. The fact is, I was heartbroken and could not bear to face what had happened. Grieving for the innocent young woman I once was, I felt the pangs of loneliness as I believed that there was no one to turn to when I became pregnant that first time. As a second and then a third abortion followed, my heart continued to be torn apart by losses I could not grasp and shame over the woman I thought I had become. My heart broke for the fathers of my first two children, who did not have the chance to participate in this crucial decision about their unborn children.

Eventually, I came to understand that the greatest heartbreak was the death of my three children through abortion. God had given me a natural instinct to protect my babies, not to kill them. Yet, I ended their lives to avoid the consequences of my own irresponsible behavior. I sacrificed their opportunity to experience a full life to save myself from disrupting my own. Accepting the truth—that what I had lost was human life—was a bitter pill to swallow. There was no turning back, and my heart was crushed by the loss.

Heartbreak is a normal and appropriate response for those who have undergone a tragic loss through abortion. We are not crazy, and we are not alone. Our heartbreak is a sign of our humanity. God created us with the capacity for deep human feelings, and these feelings can serve as guideposts on the road to healing. But to truly embark on the path to healing, we must take some time for self-reflection to know how our heartbreak has rooted itself in our lives. If we listen to and learn from our heartbreak, it will set us on the path toward wholeness and freedom. There is no sin too big for God to forgive, and if you draw close to him, he will draw close to you and heal your heartbreak.

REFLECTION EXERCISE

How to Listen to and Learn from Your Heartbreak

Abortion can be so hurtful that your heart can truly feel broken into many pieces. Yet, because of the secrecy and shame that surround abortion, you may be suffering through your heartbreak in silence, depriving yourself of the comfort and support needed to grieve and heal from your loss. Identifying and naming your heartbreaks is an important step.

Some of the factors that contribute to your heartbreak could include such things as: guilt, isolation, a lack of intimacy, self-doubt, or negative self-fulfilling prophecies. Perhaps you've discovered other aspects of your life that prevent you from wholeness. Reflect on any factors you can think of that have contributed to your heartbreak and label each of the pieces below with a factor. You may find it helpful to review your responses to the questions in Chapter One to help you pinpoint areas where you are hurting.

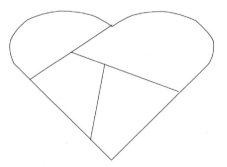

Mending your broken heart will take time, and it will take courage and perseverance on your part. But believe it or not, the heartbreak you feel after an abortion may be your first and most powerful guide into a new way of life. If you reflect on your heartbreak, you'll realize that you need help from someone greater than yourself. You need a Savior who can provide the wisdom and experiences required for your healing.

Where Can Broken Hearts Go?

God offers healing for your heartbreak through his Word:

The Lord is close to the brokenhearted;
He rescues those whose spirits are crushed.
Psalm 34:18 (NLT)

Pray:

Jesus, I did not understand the significance or the impact of my abortion, how devastating the loss would be, and how many people it would affect. My heart is broken in so many ways, and I truly desire to understand all that needs to be healed within me. I pray that you are pleased with my desire to come to grips with abortion's aftermath. Reveal to me all of the aspects of my broken heart, and help me to feel your presence as I make this healing journey. Amen.

NOTES

CHAPTER 3

CONFUSION

Definition: disorder; upheaval; tumult; chaos; lack of clearness or distinctness; perplexity; bewilderment

No one is perfect. Everyone makes mistakes. People understand that sometimes you mess up, and they are generally willing to forgive and forget. You had an abortion? Okay, that's bad, but at least you learned your lesson and will never make that mistake again. But what if you do? What if you make it not once, but two more times? Now that's really, really bad. No one can understand that. I'm not even sure I understand it myself.

The period when I was between the ages of twenty-two and thirty-two years old was a time of both great professional achievement and devastating moral failure. On one hand, I was the up-and-coming female executive in the prime of her life. On the other hand, I was a young woman caught up in a pattern of risky, promiscuous behavior that resulted in three unwanted pregnancies. What went wrong? I had not been abused, raped, or traumatized in any way. I was educated, raised in a good Catholic family, and had so many advantages. How could this have happened to me, of all people?

There are no simple answers to what seem to be such simple questions, and providing any explanation for my choices runs the risk of being interpreted as an excuse. Nonetheless, confusion about the morality of abortion and my own behavior led me to stay in denial, avoiding unbearable emotions and protecting myself from accepting responsibility for the death of my three children. Eventually, through therapy, extensive post-abortion counseling, and much prayer, I was able to think more clearly and came to understand some of the factors that made me vulnerable to abortion in the first place.

I was the youngest of four daughters and the result of an unplanned pregnancy. My oldest sister had been ill since birth, so by the time I came along, my mother was exhausted from worrying about and caring for her. Whenever I got on my mother's nerves, she had a habit of turning her back to me and commanding my sisters to "ignore!" I grew up believing that I did not matter and that my feelings were not important. As a result, I was painfully shy and socially awkward. With no brothers to guide me, and no encouragement to develop a social life, by the time I graduated from high school, I had no dates and no experience interacting with boys.

My father was quiet and rarely demonstrated any affection for my mother, my sisters, or me. Still, I adored him and earning his approval was probably the most important thing in my life. I worked hard in school to bring home good grades to please him. I tried my best to behave, but when I did something that made him angry, I was devastated. Having experienced such a distance from my mother and such little warmth and attention from my father, by the time I entered college, I was ravenous for love, respect, and attention.

I was unprepared for the freedom that was available at college. Hesitant at first, I eventually crossed all boundaries and became sexually active with my boyfriend in my junior year. I developed the mistaken belief that sex was the appropriate way to gain his attention and affection. Even though I was on the pill, I was careless about taking it, so it should not have been a surprise when I found myself pregnant a few months after graduation. Sadly, this was just the beginning of a devastating cycle of disappointment, humiliation, and despair.

You might be surprised to learn that nearly half of all women who have an abortion have two or more in their lifetime. Psychologists use the term "trauma reenactment" to explain why some women repeat their abortion experience over and over again. It is complicated and perplexing behavior, and admitting that I have had three abortions horrifies me. Dr. Theresa Burke, founder of the Rachel's Vineyard Ministries, explains, *"This problem of repeat abortions is not due to callousness or the careless use of birth control[5]."* A central aspect of trauma is a sense of helplessness, and reenactment is a way for women like me to revisit and hopefully resolve our trauma. Dr. Burke says that we repeatedly expose ourselves to the same traumatic situation in hopes that we, *"will eventually confront, conquer, and triumph over the experience, thus vanquishing the cause of their helplessness."* Eventually, I realized that forgetting the details of the events and remaining stuck in confusion were defense mechanisms that kept me in denial and unable to confront my shortcomings, grieve the profound loss of my children, or seek forgiveness.

Whether you are at a place where you can no longer avoid the pain caused by your abortion, or you finally feel up to the task of looking at your life and working through your experience, know that you are taking a step toward healing. This is called "grief work," and although it takes courage and effort to examine your own life, it produces great rewards. As your confusion and uncertainty decrease, you will be able to find meaning in your experience and a renewed sense of purpose. God wants you to live a full life, no matter what happened in your past!

REFLECTION EXERCISE

How Do You Cope?

When you experience a trauma such as abortion, you develop coping mechanisms to help you deal with all the different aspects of your distress. Some coping mechanisms are self-destructive ways of dealing with or distracting yourself from pain, such as substance abuse, compulsive overeating or dieting, promiscuity, and so on. Other coping mechanisms are neutral—they don't cause harm, but neither do they directly address or resolve the issues. These might include things like throwing yourself into your work, spending time with people you enjoy, or consciously living in the present moment. And then there are coping mechanisms that will help to set you free. These include such methods as prayer; seeking help from knowledgeable others; asking for, accepting, and granting forgiveness; letting go of irrational demands of yourself and others; and developing communication and conflict management skills.

Identify below the coping mechanisms you tend to use most frequently to deal with the various aspects of your heartbreak, whether the coping mechanism has been positive, negative, or neutral. Then list what coping skills you'd like to develop, or, if you are unsure, just note the areas where you feel you need help.

Ways I have tried to cope	How does this work or not work for you?	What will I do instead?
Example: *I avoid being around babies and young children.*	*I don't feel so bad about not having any of my own kids, but I miss out having a good time with my nieces and nephews.*	*I need to allow myself to grieve the baby I lost to abortion – perhaps by attending a Rachel's Vineyard weekend or post-abortion support group.*

Ways I have tried to cope	How does this work or not work for you?	What will I do instead?

Replacing Confusion with Wisdom

God will replace your confusion with the wisdom of his Word:

So we have not stopped praying for you since we first heard about you. We ask God to give you complete knowledge of his will and to give you spiritual wisdom and understanding. Then the way you live will always honor and please the Lord, and your lives will produce every kind of good fruit. All the while, you will grow as you learn to know God better and better.
Colossians 1:9–10 (NLT)

Pray:

I have been so confused about the past. Some things have happened that I will never forget. Other things I never want to remember. I'm trying to make sense of my abortion decision, but it is painful and, sometimes, even horrifying to think about. At the time, I thought it was the best or maybe the only thing I could do. God, I ask you to help me uncover and understand the factors that made me vulnerable to abortion. Give me courage to take responsibility for my own actions and decisions. Allow me to discover how this most difficult experience can be transformed into something good. Please let this be a way for me to know you better and draw closer to you. Amen.

NOTES

NOTES

CHAPTER 4

FEAR

Definition: a distressing emotion aroused by impending danger, evil,
pain, etc., whether the threat is real or imagined

Many complicated circumstances can lead up to and surround a woman's decision to have an abortion. Although each situation is unique, one common thread among all of our stories is how big a role fear played in our actions leading up to, during, and after the abortion experience.

Fear was a big driver in my own abortion decisions. I assumed that my mother would be unforgiving and cruel, so the prospect of facing her was dreadful. Disappointing my father was unthinkable. My older sisters were involved in their own lives, and I did not know how to begin to talk to them about what was happening. I was too embarrassed to tell any of my friends.

The fathers of my first two children never knew I was pregnant. I was afraid I would be pressured into marrying the father of my first child and the father of my second child was a man I barely knew. I'm deeply ashamed to admit that even though I did tell the father of my third child, I readily agreed to an abortion because I was afraid of losing him.

My fear didn't stop there. People knew me as a nice, smart, "good" girl, and I thought of myself that way too. So, I worried about the stigma of being an unwed mother, a consequence I was not prepared for. Believing there was no one I could turn to, my fear led me to make desperate decisions to abort my children.

As frightened as I was of what other people would think and say about me, there was nothing more terrifying about my experience than the first abortion procedure itself. I remember the feelings of sheer panic and helplessness once it started. Strangers touching me, the sucking sound of the machine, terrible cramping—these details are still vivid in my mind many years later. Fortunately, like many women, there are entire segments of time that I simply blocked from all recall, but a memory stands out of being home afterward, bleeding heavily, and enduring excruciating cramps. I was so scared, I didn't know what to do, and there was no one I could call.

Unfortunately, that was not the end of my fear. In the years that followed, I always felt uneasy that my abortions would be exposed. I worried each time I went to the doctor and had to answer the question about how many pregnancies I had. After I was married, I was afraid to have children even though my husband desperately wanted a family. Certain I would not be a good mother, I did not allow myself to become pregnant and this drove a deep wedge between us.

My greatest fear, however, was the most damaging. One abortion was bad enough, but I was terrified that three abortions were unforgivable sins. Too ashamed and hopeless to confess my mistakes and ask for forgiveness, I stopped praying and going to church. What was the point? To be honest, I did not even notice this gradual separation from God, but it lasted for a long time. Instead, I moved into the pit of self-condemnation and hopelessness.

I've come to understand that fear was a great driver in many aspects of my life. In the case of my abortions, fearfulness motivated me to make an immoral choice. It was Satan's weapon to gain control and keep me from God. He did win the battle for my soul for a period of time, but God was faithful. Just as he promises, God did not give up on me, and when I gradually, ever so slowly, reached out for help, he poured his grace into my life and revealed that I did not have to live with the fear of condemnation any longer.

When I finally understood that Jesus had gone to the cross for my sin, yes, even the sin of abortion, I had the courage to confess my sin and face its impact on my life and my babies' lives. As I began to pray more regularly and read the Bible, I drew closer to God, and his mercy and love flowed into me, replacing the fear that consumed me. It has been many years since then, and I am still challenged almost daily to live by love instead of fear. So, when worry or doubts begin to overwhelm me, I cling to God because I am certain that his love will always conquer my fear.

REFLECTION EXERCISE

Facing Your Fear

Each of us has been a prisoner of fear at one time or another. We have been afraid of loneliness, rejection, ridicule, uncertainty, violence, and even death. Fear is a powerful driver and can spur us to make both good and bad decisions. We gain a refreshed perspective when we comb through our personal histories and recall times when we have acted out of fear. By leafing through our responses to fear, we gain insight into how we can change future reactions.

Reflect back on your abortion experience. Recall the people and/or circumstances that caused you to be afraid in the time leading up to, during, and after your experience.

Example:

I was afraid of: *My mother*

What I thought would happen was: *She would be angry, ridicule me, and throw me out of the house.*

So I reacted by: *Keeping the abortion from her.*

The result was: *I did not have her support at such a difficult time, then I resented her for many years because she did not help me.*

Now, complete the following sentences for each of your fears:

I was afraid of: _____

What I thought would happen was: _____

So I reacted by: _____

The result was: _____

I was afraid of: _____

What I thought would happen was: _____

So I reacted by: _____

The result was: _____

I was afraid of: _____

What I thought would happen was: _____

So I reacted by: _____

The result was: _____

I was afraid of: _____

What I thought would happen was: _____

So I reacted by: _____

The result was: _____

Now that you have identified how fear surrounded your abortion, reflect on what you notice about yourself:

- What do your fears have in common?

- How do you typically react when you are afraid?

- What results did fear produce in your life?

- What can you learn from this that will help you when you become frightened in the future?

What God Says About Fear

God offers comfort through his Word when you are afraid:

The Lord is my light and my salvation—so why should I be afraid?
The Lord is my fortress, protecting me from danger,
so why should I tremble?
When evil people come to devour me, when my enemies and foes
attack me, they will stumble and fall. Though a mighty army sur-
rounds me, my heart will not be afraid.
Even if I am attacked, I will remain confident.
Psalm 27:1–3 (NLT)

Pray:

O God, so much of my life has been spent in fear and dread. I have allowed my fears about what other people think of me to influence my decisions. Even though the enemy wants me to believe the worst, I will not be afraid because I know that you love me, despite my involvement with abortion. Because of the sacrifice of your Son, Jesus Christ, I no longer have to be afraid of the past. I accept Jesus as my Savior and his forgiveness for my sins. I accept the perfect love of Jesus, confident that his love will quiet my fear of the future and give me courage to move on with my life. Amen.

NOTES

NOTES

CHAPTER 5

GUILT

Definition: a feeling of responsibility or remorse for some offense, crime, wrong, etc., whether real or imagined

If I told you that I felt guilty because of my abortions, you might say, "Thank goodness! At least you have a conscience." My guilt is evidence that I recognize there is a difference between right and wrong. It is a good thing that my conscience convicted me for my actions, but isn't there a point when guilt no longer serves a purpose?

I was raised by God-fearing parents who taught me that it is important to pay off your debts. Dad kept an account of whenever one of his four daughters borrowed money from him. Although he was a generous man, he wanted us to learn responsibility and to develop the discipline of paying back what we owed. My mother was gracious when she accepted a gift, but she made a mental note of it and wasn't satisfied until she had returned the favor. They were excellent role models of important values and I deeply appreciate them for it. Yet, their principles regarding debt subtly influenced my ability to accept God's forgiveness for my abortions.

My conscience kept telling me, "I owe, I owe, I owe, so I have to pay," but how could I possibly pay for taking the life of my own children? Guilt served an important purpose at that stage. It was a constant reminder of what I had done. By holding on to guilt, I could be assured that I never minimized the magnitude of my abortions. Not letting myself off the hook was my feeble way of making amends, of repaying my debt.

However, that all changed the day I read the parable of the unforgiving debtor in Matthew 18:23–35 (NIV). The story tells of a king who decides to call in the debts of all his servants. One man owed him millions of dollars but,

"He was not able to pay." Throwing himself on the mercy of the king, *"The servant's master took pity on him, canceled the debt, and let him go."*

It is true that a tremendous price had to be paid for my sins, but I did not have to pay it because Jesus already did—by his death on the cross. I cannot do anything more to make up for my abortions, including feeling bad for the rest of my life. God does not need my guilt to be added to his sacrifice. Either I believe that Jesus' death was a total and complete sacrifice for my sins, or I don't. No amount of guilt can cover up or make up for what I did. Jesus died so I could be free to forgive myself and move on with my life. The only thing I have to contribute is faith in Jesus.

I have come to understand that God gave me the gift of true remorse to point me to my sin. Then the Holy Spirit convicted me of my sin so that I could admit it, receive forgiveness, and move out of the pit of self-condemnation and guilt. However, Satan's guilt, which God did *not* put on me, was a false guilt. Its condemnation put me down and oppressed me—I felt worse. Satan did not want me to forgive myself because that would dignify what Christ did on the cross.

Whenever I am tempted to feel self-pity or to bow down to feelings of guilt, I whisper a silent prayer of thanksgiving to Jesus for relieving me of any debt I feel I owe. I choose to control my emotions, stop living by my feelings, and live by faith in Jesus.

REFLECTION EXERCISE

How Do I Cope with My Guilt?

Feelings of guilt are common among women who have had an abortion. Guilt refers to feeling bad about your behavior. You can feel guilty about things that you did as well as things that you failed to do. For example, beyond feeling guilt over ending your child's life, you may feel guilty about taking part in pro-choice activities or encouraging a loved one to have an abortion. You also may feel guilty for not telling the baby's father about your pregnancy, for withholding affection and/or sex from your husband or children, or for distancing yourself from God.

But take heart! The following pages offer practical steps for coping with and overcoming that pressing sense of guilt. The debt has been paid for your sin; it is time to move on.

Step 1

It will take time and effort to work through feelings of guilt. By answering the following questions, you can clarify how guilt stemming from your abortion has affected you and you can create a plan to move beyond overbearing emotions.

What are the behaviors or actions (things you did) related to your abortion that you feel guilty about?

What did you fail to do or say related to your abortion that you feel guilty about?

Step 2

Being honest with yourself about what you did or failed to do concerning your abortion is a very important and necessary first step in healing. The next step is to identify strategies to help you deal with feelings of guilt when they rise up or threaten to overwhelm you. Review the list below and check several steps you plan to take. Being prepared with an alternative behavior before guilt takes control is key.

_____TAKE RESPONSIBILITY

Accept your limitations. Take responsibility for making decisions that were wrong and hurtful to yourself and others. Accept your flaws and limitations.

_____TALK ABOUT YOUR FEELINGS OF GUILT

Talk with others about your feelings of guilt and shame. Meet with a mental health professional and/or join a post-abortion healing group such as Rachel's Vineyard. Seek out a pastor or spiritual advisor who can help you release your guilt and accept God's forgiveness.

_____GIVE YOURSELF TIME TO FEEL BETTER

Be realistic and accept the reality that it may take a good deal of time to feel less guilty. Change may come initially in small steps, such as feeling a little less guilty today than yesterday. Remember, feeling better about yourself will follow making positive changes in yourself and your lifestyle.

_____USE A TWELVE-STEP PROGRAM

Use the Twelve Steps of Alcoholics Anonymous, Narcotics Anonymous, and Overeaters Anonymous if you are currently struggling with addiction of any kind. Many of the steps directly and indirectly help an individual deal with guilt. For example, Step 5 states: *"Admitted to God, to ourselves, and to another human being the exact nature of our wrongs."* Steps 8 and 9 can guide you through better coping with how your guilt impacted your relationship with others.

____MAKE AMENDS

If guilt over your abortion has impacted how you treat your husband, children, other family members, friends, co-workers, even complete strangers, you can identify ways to make amends to them. A spiritual advisor or counselor can help you figure out if and how you might make amends to others.

____SEEK FORGIVENESS

Seek and accept forgiveness from God. Get involved in a strong Christian faith community to support your ongoing spiritual growth. If you have already revealed your abortion to those hurt by your action, you may choose to ask forgiveness for specific actions on your part.

____DON'T USE DRUGS OR ALCOHOL TO MEDICATE
OR DULL YOUR GUILTY FEELINGS

Staying clean from drugs or alcohol and avoiding other self-destructive behaviors will make you feel better about yourself so that you don't feel worse than you do now.

Step 3

Looking over your answers in Step 2, what is one step will you take to help you get over your guilt?

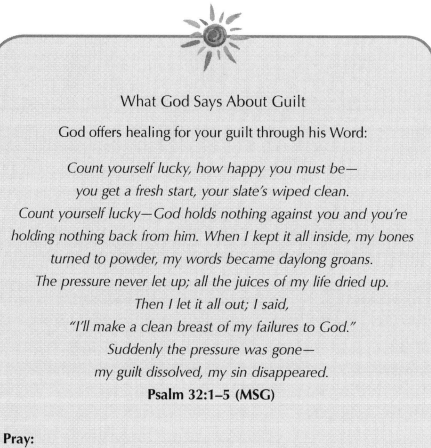

What God Says About Guilt

God offers healing for your guilt through his Word:

Count yourself lucky, how happy you must be—
you get a fresh start, your slate's wiped clean.
Count yourself lucky—God holds nothing against you and you're
holding nothing back from him. When I kept it all inside, my bones
turned to powder, my words became daylong groans.
The pressure never let up; all the juices of my life dried up.
Then I let it all out; I said,
"I'll make a clean breast of my failures to God."
Suddenly the pressure was gone—
my guilt dissolved, my sin disappeared.
Psalm 32:1–5 (MSG)

Pray:

Dear God, I want to have a proper sense of guilt for my abortion because what I did was wrong. But I know that there is nothing I can do or say that will make up for my sin. Your son, Jesus Christ, paid the price for me once and for all. Now, I choose to believe that my sin is forgiven and the debt has been paid in full. I will not allow the enemy to confuse or condemn me any longer. I refuse to let him have control of my thoughts or my emotions. I know the truth and the truth is that you have saved me and I am free! Amen.

NOTES

_____
_____
_____
_____
_____
_____
_____
_____
_____
_____
_____
_____
_____
_____
_____
_____
_____
_____
_____
_____
_____
_____

NOTES

CHAPTER 6

SHAME

*Definition: the painful feeling arising from the consciousness of
something dishonorable or improper*

Every weekend in the summertime an old pickup truck stops in a popular community park where hundreds of walkers and joggers pass by. Propped against the tailgate is a sign that reads *"Abortion Kills!"* During the most recent presidential election campaign, members of a right-to-life group waited at traffic lights, waving posters of aborted fetuses with the words *"Abortion is Murder!"* painted in large red letters. I recently passed by a Planned Parenthood office where protestors held signs reading, *"Planned Parenthood—the KILLING Place."*

For those of us who try to heal from our abortion experience and live the abundant life God has planned for us, these demonstrations can be personally devastating. Although the intentions of these signs are well-meaning—to prevent abortion and the problems that follow, some women may feel condemned and humiliated by these words and sink deeper into denial and shame. When shame overtakes us, we see our wrong behavior as our perceived identity—further evidence that we are flawed rather than normal human beings. Our abortion experience takes control of our lives, and our behaviors are driven by the deep down conviction that something is terribly wrong with us.

Some of us, convinced of our worthlessness, live out our lives to prove it. We become alcoholics, addicts, and criminals, hurting ourselves, our families, and friends as part of a distorted self-fulfilling prophecy. We expect people to treat us badly so we accept their mistreatment and violence as something we deserve. Shame over our body can lead to eating disorders such as anorexia and bulimia or to compulsions like cutting, workaholism, or other destructive behaviors.

On the other hand, many of us try to overcome painful feelings of inadequacy, failure, and helplessness by proving that we *do* have worth. Such women are constantly worried about what others think of them and are convinced others are judging them. We are called "perfectionists" and drive ourselves and those around us crazy trying to get everything just right.

It is important to understand that shame is not the same as guilt. John Bradshaw makes a distinction between the two. *"Guilt,"* notes Bradshaw, *"says I've done something wrong; shame says there is something wrong with me. Guilt says what I did was not good; shame says I am no good.*[6]*"* For many years after my abortions, I condemned myself not just for what I had done but for who I thought I was as a human being. By defining myself by my worst moments, I learned to think of myself as evil and unworthy rather than as normal and blemished.

This profound sense of inferiority made letting go of shame difficult. I was so rooted in my negative self-perception that I could not disclose my abortions to anyone, even to my therapist. It wasn't until I attended a Rachel's Vineyard program that I felt safe enough to expose my secrets. Something enormously powerful happened when "normal" women told their own stories and listened to mine without judgment. If I could see beyond their circumstances and see that they are still children of God, was it possible they could see me in the same way? When my shame was brought into the open and received with compassion and love by that community of suffering women, it began to lose its grip on me.

I now possess a new perspective and have come to understand, with a great sense of relief, that I am not perfect and I never will be perfect. I am human. It has been an even greater relief to know that God accepts me as I am. He does not expect me to be perfect and he can handle my sins. God knows who I am and what I have done and he loves me anyway. Reassured by his love, I now strive to see myself as a good, decent woman with inestimable worth—even when I make mistakes.

Developing a better self-image is important, yet it isn't guaranteed to survive every emotional blow we may take in life. When something happens that triggers an old memory, such as spotting a bumper sticker about abortion, I can quickly slip back into the loop of shame and self-condemnation. If I dwell there, the emotions that accompany those thoughts will influence how I feel and act, and the more I think about it, the worse I feel. So I had to learn how to control my thoughts and pay attention to my "self-talk."

Self-talk is what we say to ourselves, both silently in our mind as well as how we talk about ourselves aloud. It includes all the messages we give ourselves—both consciously and automatically—day in and day out. Nineteenth century writer James Allen wrote: *"You are today what your thoughts have brought you. You will be tomorrow where your thoughts take you."* (See Proverbs 23:7.)

Our minds tend to operate in a way to protect us by controlling our thought processes so that our behavior maintains the status quo. Sometimes that is a good thing. For example, when we think over and over about when we were hurt in a car accident, we feel fearful and are motivated to be cautious, ease up on the accelerator and slow down. Other times, when our thoughts keep churning over difficult experiences, like our abortion, we feel ashamed and then feel unworthy to enjoy a good life. I had to learn to notice when my self-talk got stuck in negative mode and exercise the self-control to consciously choose a different, more positive thought. The Reflection Exercise in this chapter is designed to help you do just that.

Most of us have problems with shame to one degree or another. There was a time when shame over my abortions served an important purpose in my healing. The pain pointed me to my deepest need to know that, despite what I had done, I was not lost. When I accepted God's forgiveness and believed that I was still loved, accepted, and valued by my Creator, my life changed forever, and I no longer felt unworthy of accepting all that God has planned for my future. Knowing what I would one day do, God still chose to create me. He still allowed me to venture down the path I took, and he still calls me to journey with him toward a promising future. If he is not ashamed of me, why should I continue to be ashamed of myself?

REFLECTION EXERCISE

How Can We Heal from Our Shameful Past?

Shame can direct a lot of the behavior of women who have experienced abortion. Whether you are conscious of it or not, you can become stuck in a loop of shame-based thinking that can last a lifetime. If you choose to take steps to heal from your hurts, habits, and hang-ups, you can move forward to a better life. One step in this direction is to reexamine your beliefs and assumptions about yourself and your abortion experience.

The following exercise is designed to help you develop a new way of thinking about yourself by examining the evidence that contradicts your shame-based thinking. Your life reflects proof of your worth. What are some instances where your passions or pursuits contradict those shame-based thoughts? Several examples are included to help you get started.

Shame-based thoughts and beliefs I have about myself	Evidence that contradicts my thoughts and beliefs	My new thoughts and beliefs about myself
I am a horrible person because of my abortion	I accepted God's forgiveness and am taking steps to heal	I am a brave woman who loves God and wants to draw closer to him
I would not be a good mother	I enjoy caring for children and they like being with me	I have the capacity to be kind and loving towards children

What Can God Do with My Shame?

God offers healing from your shame through his Word:

"Come now, let's settle this," says the Lord.
"Though your sins are like scarlet,
I will make them as white as snow.
Though they are red like crimson,
I will make them as white as wool."
Isaiah 1:18 (NLT)

Pray:

Dear God, for so long the shame I have felt over my abortion has controlled me. It has kept me engaged in destructive behaviors and focused on trying to win the approval of others. I know that you always condemned the sin but never the sinner, and I am ready to accept responsibility for my own actions. Please help me to let go of the hurts, habits, and false beliefs that serve no good purpose in my life. I no longer accept the lie that my identity is defined by abortion. I reject all thoughts or words of others that I am somehow not acceptable to you. I receive your acceptance through your son, Jesus Christ. I realize that you have chosen to love me, forgive me, and fully accept me. I declare that I have worth, value, and significance because you have accepted me. On that basis, I also accept myself and open myself up to receive your unconditional love. I am ready to start living the abundant life you planned for me. Amen.

NOTES

CHAPTER 7

LONELINESS

Definition: standing apart; isolated

D o you remember the classic "Young Woman or an Old Hag" optical illusion illustration? I remember as a kid nearly going cross-eyed staring at the picture. In 1915, a cartoonist named W. E. Hill first published this drawing of a figure that was "two pictures in one." Looked at one way, you see one thing (a pretty, young girl looking away from you), but looked at another way, you see something else (an older woman looking down at the floor). The key is your perception and what you expect to see.

Not too long ago, I came across a black-and-white photograph of myself taken in 1991 for my company's annual business report. The photographer had captured the image of a professional, confident, young leader—exactly the way other people perceived me to be. But underneath the assured smile, I recognized someone quite different—a lonely woman with a devastating secret she kept all to herself.

My first abortion experience was overwhelming and I could not bring myself to tell anyone about it. As time passed, I reasoned that there really was no point in talking about it and that I should just forget it and move on. But a second and then a third abortion were so horrifying that it felt impossible to ever reveal this unspeakable part of my life. I suffered alone with memories of my abortion experiences and the loss of my three children heavy on my heart.

Not having anyone to talk to about what had happened was terrible for me. I felt different from other women, and as my college friends began to have children, I pulled away from them. Convinced that I needed a lot of time alone to vegetate and relieve job pressures, I preferred to stay at home by myself instead of going out with my husband and friends. Even in the midst of the best party or family celebration, I felt disconnected from everyone else in the room. It was as if I had stepped outside of myself and was watching and listening from a distance. Caught in a vicious cycle, I isolated myself more and more, which resulted in even more loneliness. The lonelier I felt, the more I withdrew from my relationships.

Christian author and speaker Joyce Meyer suggests that loneliness is a result of not liking ourselves more than it is about not having people around us[7]. She believes that our fears about ourselves as well as our fear of disapproval and rejection keep us behind walls in an effort to protect ourselves and avoid emotional pain. I believe this was true for me.

Withholding the truth about my abortions was the only way I knew to protect myself from further pain. Unfortunately, that meant I also missed out on gaining support from family and friends. My healing was limited by my own ability to process my feelings and regroup from the trauma I experienced. Isolating myself added to the emotional damage.

Those years of unexplained loneliness make perfect sense to me now because now I understand that something was missing from my life—my children. No amount of financial or professional success can be a substitute for the relationship between a mother and her child. Three times I was given an opportunity to love and nurture another human being in this extraordinary way. There is no replacing what I have lost, and there will always be a void in my life as a result. But I have been able to find comfort in my relationship with God.

During those years when I separated from my Heavenly Father, he never left me. But guilt and shame over my abortions stood between us and I turned away from him. Of course, even though I felt alone, I was not alone. God was always there waiting for me to share my hurts, fears, frustrations, and discouragements with him in prayer. I learned to allow the pain of my loneliness to deepen my relationship with him and to use it as an opportunity to learn, grow, and mature in my relationships with others.

Isolation only leads to despair. By connecting yourself to others, you can develop trusting and fulfilling relationships that will sustain the tides of life's struggles.

REFLECTION EXERCISE

How Can I Overcome Feelings of Loneliness?

Admitting that we are lonely requires us to be vulnerable in a way that might be uncomfortable. Yet, acknowledging painful feelings is a way to process and move beyond them. Complete the sentences below with your experiences of loneliness. They do not have to be limited to your abortion experience.

Example:

I feel lonely because…*There isn't anyone I can talk to about my abortion.*

I feel lonely because…*I really don't have any close friends.*

I feel lonely because…

I feel lonely because…

I feel lonely because…

Next, consider the ways that you isolate or separate yourself from other people or activities. How does that behavior help or hurt you?

Example:

One way I isolate myself is… *I don't call my friends to do things with me.*

One way I isolate myself is… *I stay busy all the time.*

One way I isolate myself is…

One way I isolate myself is…

One way I isolate myself is…

Finally, name one action step you can take to break your isolation. How would your life be better if you did?

Example:

One step I am going to take to break my loneliness is to join the women's small group Bible study at church. This will give me a chance to meet new people and learn more about God's Word.

Your Commitment:

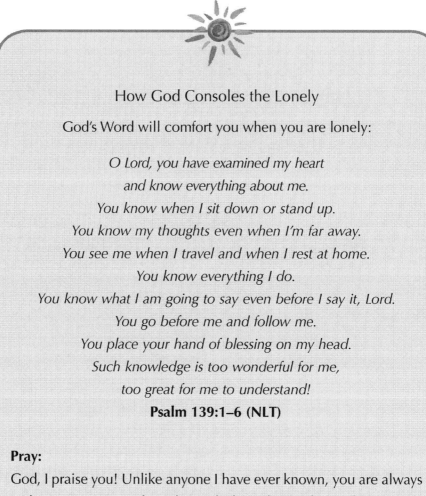

How God Consoles the Lonely

God's Word will comfort you when you are lonely:

O Lord, you have examined my heart
and know everything about me.
You know when I sit down or stand up.
You know my thoughts even when I'm far away.
You see me when I travel and when I rest at home.
You know everything I do.
You know what I am going to say even before I say it, Lord.
You go before me and follow me.
You place your hand of blessing on my head.
Such knowledge is too wonderful for me,
too great for me to understand!
Psalm 139:1–6 (NLT)

Pray:

God, I praise you! Unlike anyone I have ever known, you are always with me, no matter what. If I am feeling alone, I know that you are here. When I don't know what to do or who to turn to, I can talk to you. You understand everything about me, and you still love me and want the very best for me. If I sit quietly and wait for you, I can even hear you speak to me. O, God, how I need you! How I love you! Help me to take one step each day to end my loneliness and to seek out and accept the support of friends and family. Most of all, never let me separate myself from you again. Amen.

NOTES

_____
_____
_____
_____
_____
_____
_____
_____
_____
_____
_____
_____
_____
_____
_____
_____
_____
_____
_____
_____
_____
_____
_____
_____

NOTES

CHAPTER 8

RELIEF

Definition: a means or thing that relieves pain, distress, anxiety

Whenever there is a celebration, champagne is the popular luxury drink of choice. Whether it is a wedding, anniversary, birthday, or other special event, there is magic when the bottle is opened, the cork pops out with the sound of a bullet, and "oohs" and "ahs" resonate around the room as the foam starts spilling out of the bottle like soap suds from a washing machine. But beware! The combination of sugar and yeast produces alcohol and carbon dioxide, which builds pressure between 70 and 90 pounds per square inch-- two to three times the pressure in automobile tires! That's the reason why champagne bottles have an extremely thick cork held in place by a wire collar to withstand the intense pressure.

Being under pressure is something all too familiar to women who face an unplanned pregnancy. Nearly half of all pregnancies among American women are unplanned and four in ten of these pregnancies will end in abortion. Some might rush to judgment and draw simple conclusions about the moral character of these women. A closer look reveals that abortion decisions are often made quickly and under pressure. A combination of factors builds up to cause a woman to believe the best, and perhaps only, relief from her problem is to have an abortion.

Self image can be a big influence in abortion decisions. Some of us want to protect our "good girl" reputation for our own, and maybe our family's sake, so we allow pride and ego to sway our choice. Others, desperately trying to shed their status as a "screw-up," are convinced that having a baby out of wedlock will simply reinforce the perception that they are immature and irresponsible. We feel caught in a trap of trying to make ourselves look good, basing our decision on people pleasing, or protecting our reputation.

Other people can be compelling influencers on our decision to abort. A young girl feels powerless to defy well-meaning parents who are convinced abortion is a better option than "ruining her life" and raising a baby on her own. A husband pressures his wife to abort their fourth child because he feels stretched to the limit and overwhelmed at the prospect of one more mouth to feed. A husband or boyfriend threatens physical violence or abandonment if the woman continues the pregnancy. Even people we might have turned to for help, such as a sister or best friend, the school nurse, or a counselor, can fail us by not taking a stand and offering alternatives.

The former head of the Catholic Church, Pope John Paul II, even while condemning abortion, reached out lovingly and compassionately to women, acknowledging that, *"The decision to have an abortion is often tragic and painful for the mother.*[8]*"* He understood that many factors influence a woman's decision when she is faced with an unplanned pregnancy. He wrote, *"Sometimes the woman is subjected to such strong pressure that she feels psychologically forced to have an abortion: certainly in this case the moral responsibility lies particularly with those who have directly or indirectly obliged her to have an abortion."*

Regardless of why the decision was made, most women believe they are making the best choice at the time. Understanding the compelling reasons we chose abortion is not a means to justify or defend it. It is important so we can accept appropriate responsibility for our decision. Even though it might bring to light aspects of our character we would prefer to deny, taking personal responsibility is a key way of relieving the intense pressure that it takes to remain in denial of our experience. We may also have to face the fact that people we loved and trusted let us down, mistreated, or abused us. This knowledge, painful as it might be, can lead us to restore relationships that have been damaged or end relationships that are unhealthy or abusive.

It is a tricky thing to look back, however, because in hindsight, the reasons we chose abortion may no longer seem important, or we may wonder why we did not have the backbone to stand up to our parents, or why we did not trust others to support us. What seemed so overwhelming years ago now seems more manageable. It is both unrealistic and unfair to look back and judge the past with the experience, physical strength, and financial wherewithal we have now.

It can also be perplexing. As I reflect on my past, under the same set of circumstances I would probably make the same decisions. I remember the overwhelming panic and shame and, *at that time,* I simply did not have the emotional maturity, coping skills, or faith in God to consider any other options. At the time it felt like the right decision. So while I completely regret the choices I made, I understand and accept why I made them.

Eventually, like the bottle of fine champagne, we need to release the pressure inside so that we can enjoy the taste of a good life. I found that relief by meeting with other postabortive women and sharing my experiences. When I realized that I wasn't the only woman who was suffering from a shameful past and that other women also had multiple abortions, the relief was enormous. I was not condemned or shunned, I was comforted and consoled. Keeping my secret for so many years caused an enormous amount of pressure to build up. Now, each time I tell a part of my story, or come to a new understanding about my past, I can feel more tension release and calmness take its place.

Life presents many challenging decisions. At pivotal times in my life when I was forced to face the consequences of my behavior, I made wrong choices. I thought I was eliminating the pressures of unwanted pregnancies, but I was accepting a lifetime of pressure that abortion inevitably brings. Since for many years, I was not a believer in Jesus, I did not accept the power of his forgiveness and healing, and instead I tried to carry the burden of my emotional aftermath on my own. It took more than twenty years, a broken marriage, and a stalled career to finally force me to "uncork" the past and drink from the mercy of God—at last finding true relief from the pain.

REFLECTION EXERCISE

Expressing Your Emotions

Post-abortive women get good at building up defense mechanisms and protecting our secret. As we emotionally detach from our decision, we move on with our lives, convincing ourselves we made the right choice for that time in our lives. But the emotional aftereffects cannot be denied, so we find relief in risky behaviors, outbursts of unexplained anger or sadness, and by living a roller coaster ride of highs and lows. Others avoid pain by finding ways to desensitize themselves, often earning a reputation for being insensitive, cold, unloving, or bitchy. Relationships become a struggle where we have difficulty bonding with our husband and children, or we become overprotective and controlling.

Being able to feel and appropriately express your emotions is an important part of healing from abortion. If you do not know what you feel, it is difficult to plan how to cope when troubling feelings emerge. This Reflection Exercise will help you identify the emotions that still distress you about your abortion and help you identify some steps to brings those feelings under control.

Review the following list of emotions and circle those you have felt recently in relation to your abortion:

Abandoned	Tense	Crazy	Afraid	Angry
Crushed	Mad	Mean	Alone	Defeated
Miserable	Deserted	Troubled	Tortured	Desperate
Anxious	Guilty	Regretful	Remorseful	Betrayed
Hurt	Revengeful	Upset	Unhappy	Embarrassed
Sorry	Weary	Hopeless	Conflicted	Stupid
Jealous	Lonely	Withdrawn	Frantic	Sad

List the three emotions you often feel or that are the most difficult for you to manage:

1. _____

2. _____

3. _____

When you have those feelings, what do you do with them? Is your expression of those emotions helping or harming you?

Learning to use feelings to appropriately guide your behavior is important. What are some ways you might learn about, deal with, and express those emotions in healthy ways? Some techniques to help you with your emotions include:

1. Identify triggers that lead to the feeling, then practice "The Pause" found in Chapter 10.

2. Practice ways to deal with the feeling *before* it overcomes you. For example, you are planning to attend a friend's baby shower and you are afraid you will break into tears. You might picture yourself stepping outside to collect yourself if you become overwhelmed.

3. Find ways to help you relax. It could include things such as exercise, reading a book, cooking or baking, or talking to a good friend.

4. Keep a journal and write about your feelings. Don't worry about the quality of your writing; simply pour your heart out to release the tension or pain. If you are artistic, paint or draw a picture that conveys your emotions.

What's Next for You?

God will guide you into true relief through his Word:

Consider it a sheer gift, friends, when tests and challenges come at you from all sides. You know that under pressure, your faith-life is forced into the open and shows its true colors. So don't try to get out of anything prematurely. Let it do its work so you become mature and well-developed, not deficient in any way.
James 1:2–4 (MSG)

Pray:

God, I am ashamed that one of the emotions I had following my abortion was superficial relief. Even though I understand now why I had that feeling, I realize that it was the result of denial and not trusting you. Help me to understand my abortion experience and to learn from it so that I will become a better person. Show me how to grow in my faith and to rely on you so that I will always turn to you before making important decisions. God, you will always show me the right thing to do and offer me comfort and strength when times are difficult. In you, I can know true relief. I praise you for your faithfulness! Amen.

NOTES

NOTES

CHAPTER 9

ANGER

Definition: a strong feeling of displeasure and belligerence
aroused by a wrong

We all know what anger is, and we have all felt it—anything from a slight annoyance to full-fledged rage. Anger is a completely normal human emotion, but when not understood or properly controlled, it can lead to physical, interpersonal, and quality of life problems. The buildup of anger that commonly follows abortion can go unrecognized and unresolved for years. For those of us who deny or hide our abortions, it can be especially difficult to understand how anger might be influencing our everyday lives.

I never associated anger as a driver of some of the self-destructive behavior that followed my first abortion. But during the course of my healing process, I made an important discovery about how anger was impacting my life. The father of my third child was a married man. Our affair lasted several years, and although he never promised to divorce his wife, he encouraged me to believe it was a possibility.

When I became pregnant, I was afraid to lose him, so I hastily made arrangements for the abortion. He agreed to accompany me to the procedure but never showed up. Afterward, he said he was too busy at work and could not get away. Four months after the abortion, he took a new job and moved with his family to another part of the country. I was devastated.

Years later, during a counseling session, my therapist asked me, "Why were you so angry with yourself that you would subject yourself to this kind of treatment?" I had no answer. She went on to explain that sometimes unexpressed anger toward yourself shows up through ill-treatment by others. Did I allow myself to be disappointed and hurt because I believed I deserved it? Was my self-esteem so low that I was willing to settle for the pain and loneliness of an adulterous relationship? I began to recognize the abuse I accepted from him as a symptom of the bitterness I held against myself.

In the process of examining my interactions with others, I dug deeper to better understand the reasons for my actions, my emotions, and what I thought of myself. I soon realized that my self-perspective was rooted in rage over mistakes I made countless years ago. Haunted by my moral failures, I tried to make up for them by striving for perfection. When my attempts at perfection failed, I harbored self-resentment. The pressure I put on myself to be accepted by others kept me dependent on their love and approval as proof that I mattered.

Self-awareness was not a quick or easy process. It was frightening to get in touch with my anger because I had been conditioned to think that anger is bad. My mom had a volatile temper that petrified me, and I had vowed that I would never be like her. Certainly, some of my anger was justified and was actually a healthy response to some of my circumstances. But because I was afraid it would escalate beyond my control, I held my frustration in check, refusing to express it. Eventually, burying it had a destructive effect on my life.

Abortion is an experience that leaves many women, like me, feeling angry. Just as a small root grows up into a great tree, bitterness can develop in our hearts and overshadow our relationships. People connected to our abortion experience that we loved and trusted may have hurt or disappointed us. Others who might not have even known about it can also be the targets of our hostility. When this happens and we nurse grudges against them, jealousy, resentment, and hatred can follow.

As I later thought about my own experience, I realized that I was still furious with my parents because telling them the truth did not feel safe. I was angry with my sisters that they never noticed the trauma I had been through. I resented my ex-husband who did not know how to talk to or comfort me about the losses of my children. Although I thought I could cover up my resentments, the damage was evident in my actions towards them and people who represented them to me.

Women who have experienced abortion may have unresolved feelings of anger and bitterness towards any number of people. Some of the common targets can be: someone who pressured her into the abortion decision; herself for her promiscuity or for becoming pregnant; the father of the baby for not being there physically, emotionally, or financially; the abortion industry; God for allowing her to get pregnant or for not stopping the abortion.

I am not suggesting that every time I am angry the emotion is connected to my abortions. That would be like saying every time I am tired it is because I did not get enough sleep. With the help of a counselor who understood postabortion trauma, along with other women who shared my experience, I have explored the role anger played in my life and resolved many of those uncomfortable feelings. In the process, I have also learned and applied coping strategies that help me deal with anger when it shows up in other circumstances. Having a healthier outlook on anger has made a tremendous difference in my quality of life.

Life is full of suffering and loss, and people will frustrate and disappoint you. Things will happen that will make you mad, and sometimes fury will be justified. You cannot eliminate anger from your life altogether, but you can change the way you let people and events affect you and you can learn better ways to cope. If you feel that your anger is out of control, you might want to consider counseling to learn to handle it better. If anger tends to permeate its way into your relationships, your job, your health, or other important aspects of your life, a pastoral counselor or mental health professional can work with you to develop different tactics to relate to your anger and act on the rising emotions.

Remember that counseling, however helpful it can be, is no substitute for the wisdom of God. You can always turn directly to him in prayer and ask for his help when facing difficulties. The Bible reading and the prayer at the end of this chapter can help you get started, but you are not limited to them. Open up and tell God all that is on your heart and he will help you find freedom from destructive anger.

REFLECTION EXERCISE

Who, Me? I'm Not Angry!

When it comes to the variety of feelings involved in abortion, anger and resentment are often concealed or disguised emotions. And why not? Getting mad can be frightening and make us feel helpless. Even though we may not think of ourselves as angry, that does not mean we are not angry. Anger expresses itself in many forms, and it is important to understand the way anger shows up in your actions.

Holding on to resentment consumes a lot of physical and emotional energy. Some people are not aware of their resentful attitudes and might instead see themselves as victims. But ultimately the choice is yours—do you want to be a victim or a conqueror? Rather than dwelling on our surging resentments, we can adopt new ways of responding that can lead us to freedom and peace. Simply being aware of how much anger we feel and the circumstances that trigger it can go a long way in releasing these difficult feelings.

Complete the following three steps in this Reflection Exercise to better understand how anger affects your life:

Step 1:

Are you angry at anyone connected to your abortion experience? In the space below, describe the action or impact that is troubling you.

Step 2:

Next, describe the cost of holding on to the resentment.

Step 3:

Now, describe the benefits of letting go of the anger and resentment you are holding. How will your life be different once you do?

Example:

Step 1:

Are you angry at anyone connected to your abortion experience? In the space below, describe the action or impact that is troubling you.

My sister, Terri, was not interested at all in my life. She was so busy with her own family that she was not available to me when I needed her the most. I could not turn to her when I got pregnant.

Step 2:

Next, describe the cost of holding on to the resentment.

I don't spend time with Terri and her family. I am so angry that she has a wonderful family and I don't. I miss out on being with my niece and nephews and being a part of their lives.

Step 3:

Now, describe the benefits of letting go of the anger and resentment you are holding. How will your life be different once you do?

Instead of feeling angry and bitter, I could feel love toward my sister. Maybe that could help us get closer to one another and I would be able to confide in her more. I would be able to enjoy more time with my niece and nephews as they grow up and perhaps be a good influence on them.

Final Takeaway

On a 3 x 5 index card or small slip of paper, write the following prayer: *"God, I choose to release my anger and resentment toward (fill in the blank) and I accept your freedom in its place."* Carry this card with you or put it in a prominent place in your home or office. Repeat the affirmation daily until God speaks into your heart to change your response to this person or situation.

Your Turn:

Now it's your turn to reflect on how abortion may be the source of anger, bitterness, resentment and frustration that's ruling your life. Complete the following three step exercise:

Step 1:

List below the names or initials of anyone you are angry with connected to your abortion experience.

Step 2:

Describe the cost of holding on to resentment towards these individuals. How has it limited, complicated and or sabotaged your life?

Step 3:

What could be the benefits of letting go of the anger and bitterness you are holding? How could your life be different and better once you do so?

Final Takeaway:

On a 3 x 5 index card or small slip of paper, write the following prayer: "God, I choose to release my anger and resentment toward (name(s) of person from Step 1) and I accept your freedom in its place." Carry this card with you or put it in a prominent place in your home or office. Repeat the affirmation daily until God speaks into your heart to change your response to this person or situation.

Your Turn:

God's Word on Anger

God offers healing for your anger through his Word:

And do not bring sorrow to God's Holy Spirit by the way you live. Remember, he has identified you as his own, guaranteeing that you will be saved on the day of redemption. Get rid of all bitterness, rage, anger, harsh words, and slander, as well as all types of evil behavior. Instead, be kind to each other, tenderhearted, forgiving one another, just as God through Christ has forgiven you.
Ephesians 4:30–32 (NLT)

Pray:
Dear God, sometimes I feel things that I don't like or understand, and I don't know how to handle this. I have an especially hard time with anger. I am afraid of my anger so I sometimes I keep it bottled up inside until it explodes and hurts other people. Other times, I do not recognize my anger or I refuse to allow myself to feel it, even though it might be a signal that something is wrong. Lord, I know you created anger, along with all my other emotions. Help me to find the purpose and value of anger. Show me what I need to learn from it. Help me to release my anger in healthy ways so that I do not hurt myself or others. In the name of Jesus, I pray. Amen.

NOTES

CHAPTER 10

ANXIETY

Definition: an unpleasant state of nervousness, apprehension, fear, or worry without apparent cause

When you bake a chocolate cake, you have a pretty good idea about what it is supposed to look like, taste like, and smell like. When you sew a dress, you have a pattern to go by and a picture of the finished product. When you plant a garden, you know what to expect if you tend and care for it properly. But as you live your life, how do you know what a "good" life is supposed to look like, feel like?

I thought I had it right. I was married to a nice guy, had a fabulous career, and lived in a prestigious neighborhood. There were great vacations, plenty of friends, and money in the bank. I had nothing to worry about; yet, I was restless and keyed up all of the time. I never slept through the night and became chronically exhausted. Like annoying static on the radio, anxiety frazzled my nerves and I experienced constant edgy, nervous, unsettled feelings that I could not shake. People said that I was intense, driven, and uptight, so I chalked it up to my personality. It never occurred to me that there could be a different way to live. I made excuses for why I was never happy, blaming my husband, my boss, and my mother for why I was so worried and tense all of the time. I did not realize how much my life was controlled by anxiety until I began to understand post-abortion trauma and the effect it was having on my life.

This is a controversial topic and most women who undergo an abortion are told that there is either no psychological risk to abortion or that significant emotional problems are extremely rare. I do not remember receiving counseling or information one way or another. However, one study showed that abortion was associated with stress and anxiety two years—and even five years—after the event[9].

High levels of chronic anxiety tend to be inherited, through a combination of nature and nurture, from one's family of origin. Ann Depner, former Director of Family Services at Catholic Charities of Pittsburgh explains, *"If you have a high level of chronic anxiety, you are prone to making important decisions under the heavy influence of emotions and without the benefit of your best rational powers. This is because high anxiety impairs the rational thinking process."* Therefore, high chronic anxiety can make a person vulnerable to an impulsive abortion decision, which can lead to even more chronic anxiety.

The emotional aftermath of abortion can be so overwhelming that anxiety becomes a habitual part of a woman's life, significantly impacting her sense of well-being and ability to lead a normal life. Panic attacks, phobias and fears, obsessive-compulsive behaviors, and rituals performed to try to stop anxiety can signal that professional counseling and perhaps medication would be helpful.

Other post-abortive women I meet usually can relate to some of the same symptoms I experienced. Unable to stop my mind from racing, thoughts kept running through my head on endless repeat. Unable to relax, I had difficulty falling asleep, and then I'd awaken night after night thinking, "I can't get my mind to stop!" There would be periods of constant dread, worrying about the worst-case scenario over something that happened at work. High levels of persistent worry and chronic tension about such matters as health, money, family, or work made ordinary activities difficult or sometimes impossible. Even though there were times when I realized that my anxiety was excessive or unwarranted, I was unable to simply "snap out of it." Sometimes, just the thought of getting through the day was stressful and I suffered with some of the physical symptoms of anxiety such as fatigue, headaches, muscle tension, and gastrointestinal problems.

Given the stresses of modern life, of course it was normal to experience occasional anxiety. It was natural to worry when my father was diagnosed with pancreatic cancer, to be anxious about our finances when my husband lost his job, or to be nervous before I made an important presentation at work. Some level of anxiety helped me cope with the normal stresses of life. However, those of us who have experienced abortion often bring an already heightened state of anxiety to every situation and relationship. One of the reasons for this is the silence and isolation that typically surrounds our abortion experience, leaving no place to process our grief. Theresa Burke refers to this as "forbidden grief" and writes, *"When memories and emotions are repressed, they may come back in vague feelings or perceptions, or they may surface gradually over time as the person becomes more capable of tolerating the threat of the experience[10]."* The bottom line is that emotion that isn't dealt with shows up in a dysfunctional form in some way until we resolve the underlying issues that cause it.

It took me many years to identify that abortion was a source of my chronic anxiety, but this was not a quick and easy process. On one hand, I wanted to be free of the worry, tension, irritability, and fatigue that complicated my life. On the other hand, I was afraid of the grief I would have to face over my abortions, and I dreaded judgment, rejection, and condemnation from people I cared about. In reality, confronting the truth helped me better understand myself because I wanted to live a better life. I eventually came to accept that God wanted me to live a better life too.

Healing from anxiety involved naming and claiming the very worst part of me and the damage it had done to me and my children. That involved dismantling the secrecy of my abortions and revealing my story to others who wanted to help, not judge me. Abortion can be so overwhelming to talk about. Rachel's Vineyard helped me find my voice. It was there that I first was able to talk openly about my abortion experiences in the company of other post-abortive women. At first, it was humiliating and overwhelming. At the same time, the acceptance and support from others made it easier for me to accept God's forgiveness and to forgive myself. As that process evolved over the years, the symptoms of my anxiety began to diminish.

Of course, there are still times when I worry, cannot sleep, and feel uptight. Usually I am clear that it is not because of my abortion history but because of current circumstances, and I have learned relaxation and coping techniques that help. My greatest comfort comes through prayer and reading the Bible. When I feel anxious, I recite a Bible verse, especially the one included in this chapter. Thankfully, I usually experience immediate relief as I feel God touching my soul and reassuring me of his love and faithfulness.

REFLECTION EXERCISE

Calming Your Anxiety

According to the National Institute of Mental Health, *"Anxiety is a normal reaction to stress. It helps one deal with a tense situation in the office, study harder for an exam, keep focused on an important speech. In general, it helps one cope. But when anxiety becomes an excessive, irrational dread of everyday situations, it has become a disabling disorder.*[11]*"*

There are many ways that negative, destructive thought patterns can control our lives and steal our peace. In the process of trying to heal from abortion, it is not unusual for something or someone to trigger a memory and reset the emotional roller coaster. By understanding what those triggers are and being prepared before you react, you can calm yourself down, allowing yourself to put on the brakes, shift gears, and regroup. Without it, you might rush ahead and react before you have a chance to fully think through what you want to say or do, or remain stuck in a loop of anxiety, anger, or other destructive patterns.

Step 1: Identify Your Triggers[12]

Put a checkmark next to any of the items below that trigger your anxiety:

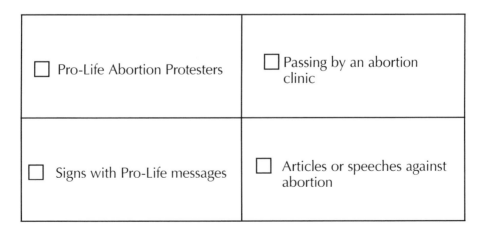

☐ Pro-Life Abortion Protesters	☐ Passing by an abortion clinic
☐ Signs with Pro-Life messages	☐ Articles or speeches against abortion

☐ The anniversary of my abortion	☐ Hearing about another woman's abortion
☐ Seeing a mother and child together	☐ Being in a doctor's office or hospital
Other:	Other:

Step 2: Breathe

To effectively engage the moment of pause, you need to have a planned and practiced technique for pausing. Use the following three steps to effectively pause:

1.   Close your mouth.

2.   Count to eight while breathing slowly and deeply through your nose. Gently let the air out through your mouth.

3.   Repeat at least ten times.

Step 3: Redirect

Make some physical movement immediately as you breathe. For example, remove your glasses, get up and stretch, shift your body weight, take a sip of coffee/water.

Step 4: Repeat

Recite a few words or a phrase you have pre-selected while breathing and performing the physical movement. Construct your phrase using information from your typical negative reactions.

Examples:

"God has forgiven me." or "God loves me." or "Let it go."

My calming phrase is:

Turning to God When You Are Anxious

God will calm your anxiety through his Word:

Do not be anxious about anything, but in everything, by prayer and petition, with thanksgiving, present your requests to God. And the peace of God, which transcends all understanding, will guard your hearts and your minds in Christ Jesus.

Philippians 4:6–7 (NIV)

Pray:

God, my loving Creator and Lord, I have been struggling for so long with worry, fear, and nervousness that I do not really know another way to be. There is so much tension in my mind that I cannot even think clearly and sometimes I can hardly breathe. The memories of my abortion are knotted up inside me. I need your help to be able to unravel my experience and face the difficult emotions churning inside of me. I know that I cannot do it alone. I am offering this prayer with the hope that you will replace my anxiety with your calm, my despair with your hope, and my tension with your peace. I pray this in the name of your Son and my Savior, Jesus Christ. Amen.

NOTES

NOTES

CHAPTER 11

ENVY

*Definition: a feeling of discontent or covetousness with regard to
another's advantages, success, possessions, etc.*

The closet in the bedroom I shared with my sister on Louise Drive
was so deep that we could conceal almost anything in its darkness.
When friends came to play, the closet was a great hide-and-seek
destination. As a teenager, I hid my diary in a shoebox in the back corner.
When the family went on vacation, Dad secured his coin collection in the
pockets of a hanging shoe bag. One day, I even found a pack of cigarettes
that my mother stowed away in an old bathrobe pocket stuffed in the back
of the closet.

Thinking about that closet reminds me of what I have kept hidden—
my envy of other people. While I worked hard at creating the image of
someone who was caring, kind, and generous, hostility lurked inside me
toward anyone who seemed to be more or have more than I. The happiness
and success of business associates, friends, family members, and even total
strangers triggered embarrassing feelings that I did not understand. Envying
others for their blessings seemed so irrational, yet it persisted in both my
personal and professional relationships.

At work, a sales executive and I were constantly at odds. People were
drawn to him and I resented his popularity. When I learned of a friend's
promotion, I congratulated her but gossiped about her failing marriage.
Devout church members made me angry, so did stay-at-home moms and
couples in love. I am ashamed to admit that I often regarded good people
with contempt, as if their happiness came at my expense.

Of all the emotions I have associated with my abortion experience, coming to grips with these particular feelings has been among the most challenging. It was not until I was nearly finished writing this book that God revealed to me that envy was the root of this problem.

Envy often gets confused with greed and jealousy. Episcopal priest and psychoanalyst Alan Chisholm explains, *"Unlike greed, which seeks to possess the good thing someone else has, or jealousy, which fears to lose the love or the good thing one has to another, envy is pained at what another person has and desires to spoil it.*[13]*"* Envy is associated with a feeling of emptiness and the need to regain some internal balance by denigrating the goodness (the intelligence, kindness, wealth, etc.) of another person. Those of us who struggle with envy are prone to one-upmanship behavior, driving ourselves crazy to outdo or keep ahead of one another.

Being unusually uncomfortable receiving gifts or compliments can be a reflection of envy. Chisholm elaborates, *"My cup is empty; I can't tolerate the fullness of yours, so I spoil it. Destructive envy represents an urgent need to spoil so as not to have to experience the pain of lack."*

This unique explanation led me to ask a tough question: "Why do I feel so empty and worthless that I want other people to feel as bad as I do?" Searching for the answer, I looked back over my life, revisiting early family experiences that caused me to feel invisible. I reconstructed my relationship history and faced the fact that so many promiscuous relationships had degraded me and depleted my self-esteem. Of course, I could not overlook three humiliating abortion procedures, and the realization that I had sacrificed my own children to protect myself was demoralizing.

Some people will say that it does no good to look back or look inside. Often their intentions are well-meaning; they want to protect you from pain. And it is true that if you are not careful you can get stuck in the past, reliving your mistakes over and over again. Yet coming to grips with my past enabled me to understand how my co-worker's popularity shined the light on my own loneliness, how a friend's success contrasted with my moral failures, and how anyone's happiness intensified my heartache. I began to see how envy took the place in my heart where compassion, love, joy, peace, and hope should have lived.

Saint Paul describes two forces fighting within each one of us—the Holy Spirit versus our sinful nature. Left to my own devices, I lived most to satisfy myself: my needs, my goals, and my wants. Relying on just my own ability to manage my life, I made numerous wrong choices. But that is not the end of the story. When I humbled myself and turned to Jesus for help and forgiveness, he blessed me with the power of the Holy Spirit to guide and protect me. After I agreed to turn over control of my life to the Holy Spirit, he began to rebuild my character in the nature of Christ. Paul tells us that when the Holy Spirit is in control, he will produce in us the qualities of love, joy, peace, patience, kindness, gentleness, goodness, faithfulness, and self-control (Galatians 5:22–23). This "fruit of the Spirit" has changed me, and since embracing these fruits, I rarely struggle with envious feelings towards others.

It is important to pay attention to your feelings, even the difficult ones like envy. The discomfort we feel signals something amiss within us that needs to be addressed. It may be that we need to change something. It can also be, as in my case, a signal that something is missing. I was lacking a spiritual leader to guide and control my life. Now when I am tempted to compare myself to others and envy what they have that I do not, I pray to Jesus. His example is my inspiration to do my best, and his loving acceptance comforts me when I fall short in any way.

REFLECTION EXERCISE

Replacing Envy with Gratitude

Envy is as old as time. Cain envied his brother Abel. King Saul envied David's accomplishments. The Jewish leaders envied Jesus' popularity. God's disciples argued over who was the greatest. On and on it goes throughout history leading up to present time. We envy a co-worker who gets a promotion, a friend who owns a beautiful home, a church member that other women admire. *Why them? Why not me?*

Envy impacts relationships and our ability to love others. St. Paul writes, *"Love is patient, love is kind. It does not envy"* (1 Cor 13:4; NIV). But something even greater is at stake: our relationship with God. Those of us who struggle with envy cannot seem to accept his grace and his blessings. The result is that we live feeling unloved and unlovable.

How can we heal from envy and cultivate a loving spirit? The answer is to nurture awareness of our blessings and develop a spirit of gratitude for them. The age-old advice to "count your blessings" is what is called for because when we focus on the good things in our life, we become less concerned about what other people have.

This Reflection Exercise is designed to start you thinking about the positive things about you and the blessings in your life. On a separate piece of paper, write out the answer to the following questions:

1. What talents or skills do you have that are helpful to others, such as being a good listener, a great teacher, a loving caregiver?

2. What is a strength that stands out? You might have a great sense of humor or a way of putting people at ease.

3. What personality trait do you have that others appreciate? For example, you may be admired for your strength, your warmth, or your imagination.

4. In what areas do people ask for your help or advice?

5. How has your ability to face and overcome adversity, a crisis, or major disappointment made you a better person?

6. What do you most appreciate about yourself? What makes you different than others?

7. Count your blessings—no fooling! For what are you most grateful? Include blessings from the past as well as the present.

There is not a quick fix to eliminate envious feelings. Yet, change can happen over time if you make a serious effort to cultivate a spirit of gratitude and grace. Stop counting lacks, insults, and hurts and make a conscious and intentional effort to count your blessings and to live gratefully.

What God Says About Envy

Allow God to replace feelings of envy with the fruit of the Holy Spirit through his Word:

Since this is the kind of life we have chosen, the life of the Spirit, let us make sure that we do not just hold it as an idea in our heads or a sentiment in our hearts, but work out its implications in every detail of our lives. That means we will not compare ourselves with each other as if one of us were better and another worse. We have far more interesting things to do with our lives.
Each of us is an original.
Galatians 5:25-26 (MSG)

Pray:
God, I pray that you will guide how I think and what I say in every moment of my life. Change my heart, Lord, especially towards those who seem to have it better than I do. Help me to rest in the knowledge that you created me and that I am valuable to you. Please release me from the envy I feel toward [names] and give me new thoughts about them that would please you. Amen.

NOTES

NOTES

CHAPTER 12

REGRET

Definition: a feeling of sorrow or remorse for a fault,
act, loss, disappointment

I t is late October, a beautiful autumn day in Pittsburgh, Pennsylvania. Once again, it is that time of year, the same season when, thirty-one years ago, I learned I was pregnant with my first child. The restless sound of the leaves and the sight of naked branches take me back to a frightening, overwhelming time, and suddenly tears flood my eyes as I am overcome with emotion. Despite the incredible healing that has occurred over many years since my abortion, regret lingers, stirred up especially at this time of year.

My very deepest regret is the fact that my abortions ended the lives of three human beings, each one with inestimable value. Their lives were lost, and I forfeited the blessing God had prepared for me as their mother. I have so many questions about what my children might have looked like, whether their personalities would have been like mine, what interests and talents God had blessed them with. I will never know the kind of mother I would have been and what our relationship might have been like. I am sure there would have been tough moments as there are between most mothers and children, but I wish I had taken the chance. I am sure I forfeited the opportunity for much love and joy.

My abortions also took a toll on many other people. Because I didn't understand the damage my action had on me, I, in turn, did not develop a proper sense of the pain or harm that could result from my behavior. I entered into romantic relationships far too quickly and ended them without remorse or empathy for the men I wounded. Perhaps the most affected was my first husband. He knew about my past before our marriage, but neither of us expected how it would affect our future together. Trust and intimacy were constant battles for me, and deeply buried feelings of self-loathing came out in bursts of rage and biting criticism, often directed toward him. While there were other problems in our marriage, I do believe that my inability to understand and manage the emotional impact of my abortions eventually contributed to our divorce, and I regret how we both suffered as a result.

The collateral damage of my abortions was not just limited to personal relationships. Unconsciously driven to rebuild my sense of self-worth, work consumed me, and career success became the measure of my happiness. My staff endured a perfectionist boss who could be relentless and hard to please. So focused on work, I allowed my family to become strangers, and I missed opportunities to influence and share in the lives of my niece and nephews as they grew up. My mother, who never knew about my abortions, took the brunt of a lot of my pain, and I treated her with contempt and disrespect far exceeding anything she deserved.

While I had come to terms with how much my abortions cost me and other people I cared about, it was at a recent women's conference when I realized that abortion took so much more. The talk around the dinner table turned to families. One by one, I listened to each woman describe her children with great pride and love. What struck me differently this time, however, was hearing stories about the sons- and daughters-in-law, the grandsons, granddaughters, even a few great-grandchildren. It was then that the full measure of what had been lost was clear. Each of my three children represented a separate branch of my family tree. Not just their lives, but the possibilities of generations to come had ended.

Imagine the human potential that is lost because of abortion: teachers to shape a new generation; scientists to discover cures for deadly disease; and leaders to bring about a safe and peaceful world. I paid a huge price for my mistakes, and so did my children. Yet what the world lost and continues to lose, with over one million abortions occurring each year, is colossal.

The list of how my abortions hurt me and others could fill many pages, and in my heart, I buried the regrets of all the things I wish I had done differently. But, of course, I cannot change the past. On good days, I even choose to be grateful for my regrets. They warn me of how much power I have to influence another human being's life—the power to love or to hurt, and my regrets remind me that my actions always have consequences. Now I try to think things through more carefully and make decisions based not just on what I think is best for me but also how they will affect other people.

Regret is a double-edged sword, and I live on the edge between what I have been and what I hope to be. It is dangerous to dwell on what I did wrong and how I hurt others because sin becomes the focus of my life rather than God's forgiveness. I regret that at the time when I desperately needed God the most, I did not have the faith to trust him. Yet, our amazing God gives me so many second chances! Now when I am tempted to berate myself for all my mistakes or when my regrets begin to overwhelm me, I ask God to protect me from despair and help me to concentrate on how my life has changed. I pray for hope for an even better future to come.

REFLECTION EXERCISE

Surrendering to Regret

We have all done things we are ashamed of, yet sometimes we get stuck in the past, reliving difficult memories. While it is valuable to reflect on our experiences, it is also important to have some clear sense of our current reality as well as a vision for the future. The following exercise will help reveal where you tend to concentrate your thoughts and offers an opportunity to make adjustments that you might find helpful.

Step 1:

During the next twenty-four hours, observe your thought and conversation patterns. At any given moment, check the focus of your speaking, listening, writing, and thinking. Is it in the past, present, or future? Also, observe the topics of your conversations and notice the balance between problems and solutions, between complaints and celebrations. Do not allow yourself to get caught up in judgment or blame; simply make a mental note of your tendency. At the end of the twenty-four-hour period, divide your day into the ways you filled your time using percentages as in the example below:

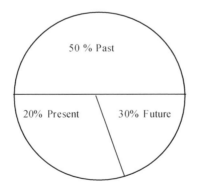

Step 2:

Describe in the space below your discoveries about where you spend your time.

Example: I spend 50 % of my time in the Past, reliving conflicts I've had and mistakes I made; 30 % of the time in the Future, worrying about my job, money, and my kids; and 20 % in the Present, thinking about what's going wrong with my day.

I spend my _____% of my time in the Past focusing on:

I spend my _____% of my time in the Present focusing on:

I spend my _____% of my time in the Future focusing on:

Step 3:

Describe any new insights you have by completing the following statements:

Example: I discovered that I really lose out on enjoying the good things happening to me in the present moment because I'm focused on the past or present. That helps to explain why I'm so uptight all the time!

Your turn:

I discovered that:

As a result, I intend to make the following changes in my thinking patterns: (Consider: What could you increase and what could you decrease that would make a difference?)

Example: I intend to spend more time recognizing the good things my kids do and less time criticizing or pointing out their mistakes.

Your turn:

I intend to… (increase)…

I intend to… (decrease)

What God Says About Regret

Find consolation from your regrets through God's Word:

There is a time for everything,
a season for every activity under heaven.
A time to cry and a time to laugh,
A time to grieve and a time to dance.
A time to search and a time to lose.
A time to keep and a time to throw away.
A time to tear and a time to mend.
A time to be quiet and a time to speak up.
A time to love and a time to hate.
A time for war and a time for peace.
Ecclesiastes 3:1, 4-8 (NLT)

Pray:

Oh, God! I have done so many things that are wrong and hurtful to me and other people. I deeply regret it all. You are an understanding, compassionate, and forgiving God, powerful enough to forgive all my sins and to take away the burdens from the past. So I release them to you now. It is time to move forward with my life, and I believe that from this moment on the emotion of regret will no longer control me. Help me to obey you and find freedom from the burden of regret. God, I love you and thank you for your unfailing love and faithfulness. Amen.

NOTES

CHAPTER 13

COURAGE

Definition: the quality of mind or spirit that enables a person to face difficulty, danger, or pain

Courage is a quality most often associated with acts of the high and mighty: missionaries, soldiers, cancer patients. Most people would not connect courage in any way with people who chose to end the life of their child, for it is true that abortion is driven largely by feelings of fear and helplessness—polar opposites of courage.

To be totally honest, when I learned I was pregnant, my greatest fear was that my sexual sin would be exposed and that people I loved and respected would be ashamed of me. The brave thing to do would have been to face the truth and to either accept responsibility for raising my children or find them a good home through adoption. By trying to cover up my promiscuity, I chose to protect my reputation rather than my children.

Sexual sin is incredibly prevalent in today's society, yet few understand the repercussions of sexual vulnerability. My sex life started in college. A prescription for birth control pills was my protection, or so I thought, from unplanned pregnancy. I had no idea that becoming sexually active at an early age and having many different partners would have such a profound and long-term harmful impact on my life and others.

Unfortunately, remembering to take my pills was a problem, and it felt awkward to ask my partner to use protection. Even after the first, and then the second abortion, I continued to engage in irresponsible behavior that put my health and the life of my unborn child at risk. Although God warns us over and over in the Bible not to have sex outside of marriage, I thought that was old-fashioned advice; I was confident I could handle myself. *What was the big deal?*

As it turns out, sex outside of marriage IS a big deal. Barbara Wilson, expert in sexual healing, explains, *"When you participate in a sexual relationship, whether you wait until you're married or not, your relationship with your partner changes. You have just possessed one another in the most intimate way humanly possible. And it impacts your entire being to the core—spiritually, emotionally, and mentally.[14]"* That explanation helped me understand my own sexual history better. For the first time, I saw that I had been craving love and intimacy with my partners and sex made me *feel* close even though there was no real love between us. A "sexual bond" was created and, as one after another relationship ended, I was left damaged, wounded, and the mother of three aborted children.

Whether it was my forgetfulness, immaturity, or failed birth control that resulted in pregnancy, it really does not matter. The fact remains, I never would have become pregnant if I was not fooling around. It is not easy to confront this aspect of my character, but after years of soul-searching, I finally had the courage to accept that I was wrong to deny my sexual sin, make up excuses, and rationalize my behavior.

Pastor Tim Keller said, *"Remember the two sides of the gospel message: you are more wicked than you ever dared believed, and you are more loved than you ever dared hoped.[15]"* That was an encouraging message as I confronted my lifestyle of promiscuity and broke off destructive relationships. I have confessed my sexual sin and know that I have been forgiven. To ensure I have the best relationship possible with my husband, I have examined the impact of past sexual bonds and I have taken steps to break them.

I read somewhere that the opposite of faith is fear. That makes sense to me now. As I drew closer to God, I found the courage to take additional, sometimes shaky steps toward full healing and restoration. Deeply entrenched habits that had numbed my pain were broken, including my addiction to cigarettes, alcohol, and overwork. The task of dismantling a life built to protect myself and then rebuilding my life was enormous, and it continues to this day.

God blessed me with a voice to speak out about my abortions and spread the word of his grace and mercy. I have become bolder, creating a website and speaking publically about my emotional and spiritual transformation. The reception has not always been warm. Usually, people are uncomfortable with the topic of abortion—they do not seem to know what to say. Some are outspoken and judgmental, exclaiming, "I don't know how a woman could ever kill her own child!" But others recognize that we are all sinners and respond with compassion.

If you are wondering whether you should tell people about your abortion, my best advice is to pray about it. It is a decision that most of us struggle with from time to time. Some women choose to be public about their experience and join anti-abortion campaigns like "Silent No More." Others keep it a private matter between immediate family and a few close friends. There is no right or wrong answer to the question, "Should I tell?" It is a personal decision. It probably will not be easy to tell your husband or a serious dating partner, but whatever God puts on your heart to share, he will carry you through it.

Whether you choose to tell other family members or friends about your abortion is up to you, and it may be helpful to consider the following questions: What do you hope to gain by disclosing your abortion? Who needs to know? How will the knowledge benefit the other person? What are your fears about telling them? Are you prepared for a negative reaction?

If you have lived to protect your abortion secret, telling may seem like a huge risk. Seek advice from people you trust and know that God will give you the courage to share your story with others at the proper time and the strength to handle whatever follows.

So courage is connected with abortion after all, perhaps in unexpected ways. Never underestimate your courage to confront and heal from your past and the strength you possess to rebuild from the choices you have made. However, do not believe for a second that you can do this on your own power. Your healing requires the heavy-duty and everlasting strength of our God, and it will be there in an instant—all you have to do is ask for it!

It took courage to buy a book on abortion healing and risk being "discovered" somehow. It was brave to open the book, to read the words that convicted you or revealed your deepest shame and hurt. It will take courage to make the next step, and then the next one and the one after that. I applaud your courage. So does God. He is rejoicing right now at how brave you are!

REFLECTION EXERCISE

Real Courage

Courage is like a muscle. The more you exercise it, the stronger it gets. Reflect on the times when you have shown courage. You might remember a time in junior high school when you stood up for a friend or made a career change later in life. Maybe you ended an abusive relationship and had to strike out on your own. Make notes of several examples below:

-

-

-

Review these examples and ask yourself the following questions:

1. How and when did you show determination and courage to eventually succeed or overcome the situation?

2. What strengths were you able to use in that situation?

3. What was the outcome?

4. How did your faith help you?

5. What can you learn about yourself from the times you acted with courage?

6. What next step do you need to take in healing from abortion? What do you need to take that step? How can you draw from the times you have been brave in the past to help in future situations?

What God Says About Courage

Allow God to give you the courage to heal through his Word:

Be strong. Take courage. Don't be intimidated. Don't give them a
second thought because God, your God, is striding ahead of you.
He's right there with you.
He won't let you down; he won't leave you.
Deuteronomy 31:6 (MSG)

Pray:

God, I need to draw on your courage right now because I am afraid about (name your fear). I want to do the right thing no matter what happens or what other people might think or say. Please help me to take the focus off myself, my fears, my plans, and my desires and fix my eyes on you and what you want in this situation. If I do that, I am confident that you will not fail me and will help me. Oh, God, how I love your wisdom and strength! Thank you for helping me! Amen.

NOTES

NOTES

CHAPTER 14

LOVE

Definition: a profoundly tender, passionate affection for another person

Like many little girls, I played with dolls and pictured the day when I would get married and have my own babies. In my fantasy, my husband would be Tom, the cutest boy in second grade. I would have two daughters, Linda and Kathleen, named for my sisters' prettiest girlfriends. My dream stayed intact through high school when I did a lot of babysitting, especially taking care of infants and toddlers. I always assumed that after college graduation I would marry, have children, and become a stay-at-home mom, loving and raising my family.

Reality, of course, was quite different for me. When I became pregnant, my natural instincts to love and protect my child were stifled by fear and shame. Reacting from those difficult emotions, I began a cycle of repeat abortions and, by the time I was thirty-two, my dream of becoming a mother was over. Even though I married and promised in my wedding vows to accept children, I never allowed myself to become pregnant again. When asked whether I wanted a baby, I would respond with a fervent, "No! I would be a terrible mother." After what I had done, I had absolutely no confidence in my ability to protect and care for a baby. Maybe on some level, I was even afraid I would choose another abortion.

Of all the ways that abortion hurt me, the most devastating effect is that I will never know what it is like to be a mother. Aborting my own children and then avoiding pregnancy later robbed me of the chance to give and receive love in that very unique and profound way.

Instead of nurturing my capacity to love, with each abortion I became tougher and more cynical and my ability to feel profound emotions such as compassion and affection seemed to dry up. There are no words that can heal a broken heart that is closed by pain. Only the power of love can change it. Shutting down to protect myself, consciously or unconsciously, I had to learn to let go of guilt, regret, shame, and other trying emotions so that love could come and take their place in my heart.

It took a long, long time, but the starting point came as soon as I accepted mercy from Jesus. As I began to understand his unconditional love for me, my heart began to soften. Later, as I ministered to other women and men who had experienced abortion—listening to their suffering, sharing their grief, understanding their loss, my capacity to love others began to grow.

After my divorce, I believed that I would go through life without knowing the love that could be found in a solid marriage. However, God blessed me with Bill, my second husband. My heart overflows with love for him, and my great joy is believing how much he loves me too. This relationship is precious to both of us, and we strive to keep Christ in the center of everything we do.

As it turns out, God had even greater blessings in store for me. Earlier this year, I was praying for my ninety-two-year-old mother who was dying from cancer and old age. Compassion for her suddenly overwhelmed me, and I could not stop crying, thinking about all of the anger and bitterness I felt toward her during my lifetime. I was stunned by new, tender feelings and resolved to love her as I had longed to do my entire life. In the months that followed, we enjoyed being together and seemed to reach a new understanding of one another. Because I accepted God's grace, Mom finally knew that I loved her and that my heart had changed.

We are created for relationships, not isolation; for intimacy, not loneliness. None of us are unlovable or incapable of loving. It took me many years to see this, but when I did, things were never the same again! God is *"merciful and compassionate, slow to get angry and filled with unfailing love,"* says Joel 2:13 (NLT), and God teaches us that the best thing we can do is to love him and love one another as we love ourselves. My abortions never changed God's love for me, and I never lost the capacity to love others, but the enemy used my abortions to trick me into believing otherwise. Now I realize that God never expects us to give something away that we do not have. So he loves us first and expects us to let his love flow through us to other people.

REFLECTION EXERCISE

My Capacity for Love

1. How has your capacity to love other people been impacted by abortion? How has it affected your ability to love yourself?

2. How has your capacity to receive love from other people been impacted by abortion?

3. What attitudes and behaviors should you examine and perhaps change to be more loving and accepting of love from others?

4. Perhaps you need to begin by being more loving toward yourself. What step could you take to be more loving, kind, and compassionate toward yourself?

5. Who do you need to forgive? What is one step you could take in the direction of reconciliation?

God Is Love

Experience the healing power of God's love through his Word:

When I think of all this, I fall to my knees and pray to the Father, the Creator of everything in heaven and on earth. I pray that from his glorious, unlimited resources he will empower you with inner strength through his Spirit. Then Christ will make his home in your hearts as you trust in him. Your roots will grow down into God's love and keep you strong. And may you have the power to understand, as all God's people should, how wide, how long, how high, and how deep his love is. May you experience the love of Christ, though it is too great to understand fully. Then you will be made complete with all the fullness of life and power that comes from God.

Ephesians 3:14-19 (NLT)

Pray:

God, you loved me before I was even born and you have never stopped, no matter what I have done. I refuse to believe any person or hold any thought that might suggest I am not worthy of your love. I am your child, created in your image. You love me and I need your love, I want your love, I accept your love!

I accept responsibility for those things I have done or said that have caused trouble in my relationships. If there is anything in my life holding me back from loving other people as you have commanded me to do, I pray that you will reveal it to me now. Help me to grow in patience, compassion, and kindness toward others, especially (name).

God of infinite love, today I put aside hard feelings, grudges, or feelings of unworthiness that have become barriers to my ability to accept the love of good people for me. Thank you for the blessing of all the people who love and care for me. Amen.

NOTES

_____

_____

_____

_____

_____

_____

_____

_____

_____

_____

_____

_____

_____

_____

_____

_____

_____

_____

_____

_____

_____

_____

CHAPTER 15

PEACE

Definition: freedom of the mind from annoyance, distraction, or anxiety

Each year, on the second Sunday of May, Mother's Day celebrations unite families across the nation. President Woodrow Wilson first declared this national holiday in 1914 as an opportunity for American citizens to honor those mothers whose sons had died in war. Almost one hundred years later, it is still a time to recognize the bond between mother and child. Ministers and priests use this day to pray for mothers, praising them for the sacrifices they make. Children are reminded of the fifth commandment and are instructed to love and honor their mothers. In churches all across the country, mothers will stand, be acknowledged, and receive a blessing.

However, each Mother's Day millions of other women who have experienced abortion will remain seated, feeling unable and unworthy to claim our children because of what we did to end their lives. On this holiday, our loss feels particularly real because we have no child to hold in our arms or smile at with love and pride. We have no son, no daughter to give us flowers or take us to Sunday brunch. But that does not mean we won't be missing and loving our children, longing to see them, to hold them, to talk to them, to know them, and to be known by them.

I will never forget the moment when the realization that I had aborted my very own children fully hit me. It was during the naming ceremony in the Rachel's Vineyard program, and I was mere minutes away from having to announce the names of my children. Up to that point, I really had no sense of them as human beings let alone whether they were boys or girls. When the time arrived to speak their names, I was in anguish because I knew in my heart that by giving each a name I acknowledged that they did exist and that I was their mother. I was beside myself, sobbing uncontrollably as I finally blurted out the names, *Ann, James, Jane.*

It was a traumatic, unforgettable moment. This seemingly simple act of naming my children was a turning point. With their names, I acknowledged and restored their dignity as human beings and fulfilled my sacred responsibility as their mother. Afterward, I began to examine my life, face the hard truths of things I regretted doing and was ashamed of, mourned my losses and missed opportunities, and at last, repented of my sins and the suffering they caused. God honored my acts of humility and obedience, and transformation within me began.

Gradually, over the past ten years, my children have become more real to me, and I have developed a relationship—a spiritual relationship—with them. I sometimes wondered, "Are my babies in heaven?" and "Will I ever see them?" Pastor and teacher John MacArthur offers encouraging insight into what happens to children—unborn, stillborn, infants, and young children—when they die. His conclusions are based on careful research of Holy Scripture rather than on hopeful emotion. He writes, *"All children who die live in the presence of the Lord for all eternity. They are blessed forever in their death!*[16]*"* Furthermore, those of us who have accepted God's forgiveness and placed our faith in Jesus, living in such a way that reflects this change of heart, can be encouraged. MacArthur reminds us of the Good News: *"Your joy in anticipating a reunion with your little one who dies is dependent on your knowing you are going to the place where he or she is. Your child will greet you in eternity one day only if you have believed and received Jesus Christ as your personal Savior.*[17]*"*

It is no exaggeration to say that I never knew a peaceful moment after my first abortion. My life was forever changed and filled with anxiety and pain. Now, thankful that I am saved, I finally enjoy a life that is mostly calm and peaceful. I am so grateful to know that Ann, James, and Jane are my children and that I am their mother. Now, each Mother's Day, I thank God for his abundant grace that has allowed me to know them and for his promise that later I will finally be united with them for eternity.

REFLECTION EXERCISE

A Letter to Your Child

The following exercise is for the purpose of coming to know your child that has been lost to abortion and finding peace in that relationship. Begin with prayer, asking God to help you get a sense of your child. Give your child a name. What do you want your child to know about you? Tell your child all that is in your heart right now as his or her mother. If you have lost more than one child, you may prefer to write a separate letter to each of your children. The following sentence-starters are offered to guide your reflection:

Dear _____,

I want you to know that…

I made the decision for abortion because…

What I didn't know or understand at the time was…

I hope you will understand that…

Your father…

What I miss most about you is…

I will always…

When I see you in heaven I…

I promise…

Love,

Your Mother, (insert your name)

The Peace of Christ

Allow God to bring you peace through his Word:

I am leaving you with a gift—peace of mind and heart.
And the peace I give is a gift the world cannot give.
So don't be troubled or afraid.
John 14:27 (NLT)

Pray:

God, you are so amazing. You are wonderful. You are generous beyond imagination. You are great. You are so good to me. You are my heavenly Father, and I love you so much. From this moment on, I release all of my anxiety, worry, regret, shame, guilt, resentment, anger, bitterness, heartache, and loneliness. I ask you to take back any ground that I have yielded to the devil's control due to my sin. I give you my soul completely, and I receive your peace now, in Jesus' name. Amen.

NOTES

NOTES

CHAPTER 16

FREEDOM

Definition: personal liberty, as opposed to bondage or slavery; the power to exercise choice and make decisions without constraint from within or without

L ooking back over the last twenty-five years, I almost cannot believe that this was my life! Now I recognize how the decisions I made and the actions I took so powerfully shaped the course of my life. But at the time, it was not so clear to me. It is tempting to play the "what if" game, remembering key turning points and wondering: "If I had made a different choice, how would my life be different today?"

Of course, I will never know the answer to that question, but I imagine that it would have been a much better life. I imagine that without the stigma of abortion lurking in my past, I would have been free. Free from trying to prove I was perfect. Free from degrading, sexual promiscuity. Free from drinking and smoking to numb the pain and calm my nerves. Free from the fear of letting people get too close. Instead, I defined myself by what I had done and lived within the limits of what I thought I deserved—my own personal hell.

In Jesus' time, someone who couldn't pay a debt was thrown into prison until the obligation was satisfied. If no one came forward to pay the debt for the prisoner, he or she would probably die there. Serving as my own judge and jury, I condemned myself for my abortions and spent my life trying to pay off my sin debt. It was not clear to me that no amount of professional success or volunteer work or self-improvement study could overcome my sense of inadequacy and unworthiness.

My healing journey has led me to understand that Jesus freed me from this invisible prison and from the consequences of my sin when he died on the cross. His redemption offered me the choice to follow him and create a different quality of life. Jesus' sacrifice freed me to become all that God meant for me to be.

Freedom was wonderful, but it also posed new challenges. My life did not instantly change. I was like many ex-convicts released from prison who have a hard time readjusting to freedom and functioning in a world without bars, structures, and limits. I was addicted to work, hiding in the stress and pressure to avoid dealing with my problems. Once freed from guilt, my sense of identity was challenged, throwing me into personal and career crises. If I was no longer the sinner suffering from abortion, who was I and what was next for me? I quit my job, then floundered for several years, trying to find my way professionally.

Bigger obstacles developed in my relationships. I had hurt people with my angry and contemptuous behavior and was not able to repair some of the damage. My marriage crumbled and ended in divorce. I began another romantic relationship, but eventually recognized I had fallen into old patterns of sexual sin, hoping to find love with the wrong man.

My emotional and spiritual growth was a long process with many ups and downs. I was a work-in-process but finally, amazingly, freed from sin and its stronghold on my attitude, actions, and emotions. It was up to me to rebuild my life and make changes. Yet, freedom was strangely frightening. Just as former inmates, each new day offered me the opportunity to make conscious and intentional choices about who I wanted to be and how I was going to act. I knew I had to let go of self-imposed limitations, develop discipline, and form new patterns of behavior if I was going to become the woman God created me to be.

One day at a time, over time, I began to make changes. I learned to fortify myself with God's Word by making a daily habit of reading the Bible. Knowing the importance of surrounding myself with people who were already successfully walking in God's way and doing his will, I joined a thriving Christian church community. I refused to date men who were not Christians, and I created new friendships with women who shared my desire to follow God.

As weeks, months, and years passed, I experienced the tangible difference that my new way of life made. I felt stronger, happier, calmer, and more clear-headed. I accepted the freedom Jesus gave me and left my prison of shame and guilt. I am now free to admit my own limitations and imperfections without self-condemnation. I am free to accept people who are different from me. I am free to forgive others as well as myself. I am free to love and be loved. I am free to serve and glorify Christ by living a full, satisfying, and happy life!

Yes, it is really okay to have a good life after abortion. You are taking steps in that direction by exploring your past and reaching for emotional and spiritual healing. There will be ups and downs, victories and defeats. I promise you that freedom from your past is worth it—beyond your wildest dreams. Do not give up. Please, do not *ever* give up!

REFLECTION EXERCISE

The Power of Letting Go and Being Free

Sin has a way of imprisoning and dominating us; it has a knack for controlling our actions and our emotions. Sin tends to keep us focused on our problems and weaknesses rather than our blessings and strengths. One of the greatest blessings God gives you once you confess your abortion and accept his forgiveness is—freedom! Sometimes the freedoms are *from* something, for example, sadness, anxiety, or addictive behaviors. Other times, the freedoms are *to* new opportunities or changed emotions. The following exercise challenges you to reflect on where you are in your healing journey from abortion. What damaging emotions or activities have you found freedom from, and what does this enable you to be free to do? Using the example below, complete your own list of freedoms.

I am free from:	I am free to:
Crushing grief and loneliness	Reach out and make new friends
The anxiety of hiding my "secret"	Allow myself to become pregnant

Reflection Question: What is possible for you now that you are free?

The Price of Your Freedom Has Been Paid!

Accept the freedom of God's Word:

For he has rescued us from the kingdom of darkness
and transferred us into the Kingdom of his dear Son,
who purchased our freedom and forgave our sins.
Colossians 1:13-14 (NLT)

Pray:

God, I let go of the thoughts, beliefs, and behaviors that have imprisoned me in guilt and shame. I am free from all that separates me from you and keeps me in an empty, unfulfilling life. I accept Jesus Christ as my Savior and believe that I have been fully forgiven for all of my sins and the sin of abortion in particular. I release the past, and today I start a brand new life. From this point forward, I am free to love others fully. I am free to build a good life. I am free to grow closer to you every day. Praise God, I am FREE! Amen.

NOTES

CHAPTER 17

GRATITUDE

Definition: a feeling of thankfulness and appreciation

Over coffee at Panera's, a friend of mine who read a draft of this book remarked, "You've really come a long way, haven't you, Jane?" My automatic response was, "Yeah, but I still have such a long way to go. One of these days, I'm really going to get my act together."

"One of these days…" That reminds me how I am always thinking that my life will be really happy "when…" It seems I am always waiting for something (or someone) to change my life for the better. Whether it is a new job, a better home, or more money, there always seems to be one more thing I want. When I finally know enough, accomplish enough, then I can have the life I really dreamed of, when, when, when…

Reflecting on our conversation that morning, I recognized how the pattern of all the "if onlys" and "when that happens" and "as soon as he or she…" keeps me from appreciating what I have right now. I overlook how God has blessed me with forgiveness and delivered me from heartbreak. What greater gift is there than God's love?

I will be forever indebted to Theresa Burke for developing the Rachel's Vineyard program and for Catholic Charities in Pittsburgh that made it available to me. I firmly believe Rachel's Vineyard saved my life.

I am thankful for the spiritual relationship I now have with my three children; they are precious to me, even though I have never been able to see, touch, hold, or talk to them. In their memory, I sometimes wear a bracelet with three silver strands and three small hearts dangling from the clasp. Touching the sterling silver charms reminds me that I am a mother, even if most people don't know it and I don't tell them.

Memorializing aborted children is not an uncommon practice. In some cemeteries there are special areas put aside where you can purchase a stone or brick with your child's name carved in it. Some women choose to wear a piece of jewelry with their child's birthstone or something engraved with the child's name or initials. If you have not participated in a memorial service for your child through a post-abortion healing program such as Rachel's Vineyard or the Forgiven and Set Free Bible Study, you might consider doing so on your own. Some women have made a donation to a favorite charity in their child's name or planted a special tree in their backyard.

At first, you might think this is strange or morbid; it may not be something you ever imagined doing. What you choose to do does not have to be anything obvious or expensive, for even the smallest gesture can bring comfort and peace. However, choosing some way to recognize that your child is real can be an important part of your healing. It is one way to demonstrate gratitude for that child's life, a token of what your child means to you.

I cannot see my children today, but I am not going to wait until "one of these days" to savor how my children have changed my life, just, I suppose, as all children change the lives of their mothers. It was through grieving their loss that I came to know my Lord and Savior. For that I am so grateful and will be for the rest of my life.

REFLECTION EXERCISE

My Daily Gratitude Journal

With all the busyness in our lives and the many challenges we face each day, it is easy to overlook the good things that happen. It can be even more difficult to find the blessings in our trials and difficulties. Could anything positive have come from your abortion? In the following exercise, you are invited to consider that question.

1. How has your abortion experience changed you? How have you grown emotionally and spiritually?

2. How has your abortion experience impacted your relationships? To whom are you especially thankful for at this point in your life?

3. What is one thing you will always treasure about your healing?

4. What have you been praying for and how have your prayers been answered?

5. What is still unresolved and what is your prayer now?

Gratitude to God

Give thanks to God by reading his Word:

Always be joyful. Never stop praying. Be thankful in all circum-
stances, for this is God's will for you who belong to Christ Jesus.
1 Thessalonians 5:16-18 (NLT)

Pray:

O, God in heaven, how I praise your holy name! You are so great and so good to me. Your blessings have enriched my life far beyond anything I deserve. How I thank you!

Dear, sweet Jesus, you gave your life for me so that I would never have to pay the price for my own sins. Your sacrifice assured me an eternal place in heaven with my children. How I thank you!

Holy Spirit, you live in me, guiding me to overcome the past and to live a life that's worthy of all the blessings I have received. Your presence is my lifeline to God the Father and unites me to his Son, Jesus. How I thank you! Amen.

CHAPTER 18

HOPE

*Definition: the feeling that what is wanted can be had
or that events will turn out for the best*

When I talk openly about how abortion affected my life, many people find it difficult to understand. Some dispute that abortion is a traumatic experience. Others fail to grasp how denial and shame so fiercely kept me from accepting God's forgiveness. The best way I can describe my healing journey is that it was like being in the midst of dense fog for a long, long time.

If you are like me, when I am driving and become surrounded by heavy fog my anxiety level goes way up. I hold my breath and search for a place to pull over, but I feel trapped because I can't even find the edge of the road. I continue cautiously, nervously, hoping to avoid an accident but expecting the worst at any minute. It is a relief to finally make out the painted yellow and white lines because now there is something to focus on to keep the car moving in the right direction on the correct side of the road. When the fog clears and I can drive on without obstruction, I relax and look forward to where I am going, confident that everything will be okay now.

Many years of my life resembled living in a fog, clouded by the terrible secret lurking in my past. For over twenty years, I could not see how three abortions had impacted my life, creating severe anxiety and depression. I was unable to see God as the merciful and loving Father that he is, and I had no hope for forgiveness. So I accepted that this was the way my life was going to be and convinced myself that it was not so bad after all.

But God did not give up on me, and thankfully he had better plans in mind for me! I came to a crossroads when I summoned the courage to attend a Rachel's Vineyard program and connect with other women who understood my distress. The living Scripture exercises and other activities helped to make my abortion experience real and tangible for me for the first time, and hearing the similarly painful stories of other women who experienced abortion smothered my feelings of isolation.

Afterward, I committed myself to studying the Bible and memorizing Scripture because I could see, hear, and experience God through his Word. As my desire for a relationship with him grew, I developed habits of attending daily church services and praying regularly. Finally, I had something solid to help me navigate through life; I had the assurance of my salvation through Christ and God's promises for my future. For the first time in my life, I felt hope and a desire for a better future.

It is amazing how hope can change your life. No longer willing to settle for work I did not enjoy as an escape or a lifestyle packed with tension and stress, I took steps to create a better life. A friend suggested that I read *The Path*[18] by Laurie Beth Jones, and when I had finished, I had a sense of purpose and an idea of God's will for my life. After turning that last page, I wrote a personal mission statement, a simple two-page description of my hopes and dreams. A plastic three-ring binder became my "Dream Book," and I filled it with photos, travel advertisements, magazine articles, a reading list, and countless other symbols that represented the life I hoped to create. With a different, better future in mind, I felt the courage to make changes in my life that started small and grew bigger and bolder over time.

In his book *Addiction and Grace*, Gerald May reminds us, *"Because of God's continuing love, the human spirit can never be completely obliterated,"* and *"There is always some level at which we can choose, freely, to turn to God or to turn away from God, to seek grace or avoid it.*[19]*"* For most of my adult life, it was better to be numb to my emotions than to feel the heartbreak of my abortions. But then I found the words of Jeremiah 29:11–14: *"For I know the plans I have for you,"* says the Lord. *"They are plans for good and not for disaster, to give you a future and a hope."* I cherished this promise as I resolved to change my lonely, unfulfilling life.

The last sentence of my mission statement reads: "Life is good and precious to me." It is now ten years since I wrote those words, and my life today is tangible proof that God heard my prayers all the way from heaven! My hopes and dreams have been fulfilled. My career as a professional business coach is exciting and rewarding. My husband is the best man I have ever known, and I love him more every day. My health is great; I have even survived breast cancer. The opportunity to care for those who suffer from postabortion pain through my Messy Miracles Ministry is an amazing gift from God. When I really think about it, healing my emotional and spiritual wounds has truly changed my life. If I could find hope in my brokenness, certainly you can too.

REFLECTION EXERCISE

God's Promises

God has a purpose and a plan for your life, and the future he has in mind for you is wonderful. Sometimes, however, our life circumstances and the consequences of our choices make it difficult to believe that a better life is possible. We can rely on God's promises when we are in need of comfort and assurance.

Review the following questions and answer them as honestly and completely as you can. Then review the promise being made to you by your loving, Heavenly Father in that area. Choose one or two that seem to speak most to your needs at this time and write a brief prayer asking God for the faith to believe and the patience to wait for him to act. Be assured to know that God loves you and he *always* keeps his promise and *always* offers hope for a better future.

Confidence: In what area of your life do you need greater self-confidence?

And I am certain that God, who began the good work within you, will continue his work until it is finally finished on the day when Christ Jesus returns. (Philippians 1:6)

Courage: How is fear controlling and holding you back?

This is my command—be strong and courageous! Do not be afraid or discouraged. For the Lord your God is with you wherever you go. (Joshua 1:9)

Forgiveness: What unforgiveness do you hold in your heart towards yourself or someone else. What do you need to be able to release it?

And I will forgive their wickedness, and I will never again remember their sins. (Hebrews 8:12)

Help: What is most troubling you? Where do you most need God's help right now?

God is our refuge and strength, always ready to help in times of trouble. (Psalm 46:1)

Hope: What are you hoping will happen? Why is it important to you?

Let us hold tightly without wavering to the hope we affirm, for God can be trusted to keep his promise. (Hebrews 10:23)

Love: What do you need to believe that God loves you, *no matter what?*

No eye has seen, no ear has heard, and no mind has imagined what God has prepared for those who love him. (1 Corinthians 2:9)

Patience: In what circumstance do you feel most impatient? What is your fear?

Patient endurance is what you need now, so that you will continue to do God's will. Then you will receive all that he has promised. (Hebrews 10:36)

Provision: What are your financial concerns?

And this same God who takes care of me will supply all your needs from his glorious riches, which have been given to us in Christ Jesus. (Philippians 4:19)

Rest and Relief: How are stress and exhaustion impacting your life?

Then Jesus said, "Come to me, all of you who are weary and carry heavy burdens, and I will give you rest. Take my yoke upon you. Let me teach you, because I am humble and gentle at heart, and you will find rest for your souls. (Matthew 11:28–29)

Strength: What area of your life do you need to turn over to God—completely?

Each time he said, "My grace is all you need. My power works best in weakness." So now I am glad to boast about my weaknesses, so that the power of Christ can work through me. (2 Corinthians 12:9)

Success: What concerns do you have about your job or work?

And may the Lord our God show us his approval and make our efforts successful. Yes, make our efforts successful! (Psalm 90:17)

Wisdom: In what area do you especially need insight or guidance from God?

If you need wisdom—if you really want to know what God wants you to do, ask him, and he will gladly tell you. He will not resent your asking. (James 1:5)

A Future Full of Hope

Discover hope in God's Word:

"For I know the plans I have for you," says the Lord. "They are plans for good and not for disaster, to give you a future and a hope. In those days when you pray, I will listen. If you look for me whole-heartedly, you will find me. I will be found by you," says the Lord. "I will end your captivity and restore your fortunes. I will gather you out of the nations where I sent you and will bring you home again to your own land."
Jeremiah 29: 11–14 (NLT)

Pray:

Dear Father God, you never cease to amaze me! No matter how far I wander away from you, you take me back. I don't want to live in darkness, on my own. Instead, today I claim all of the promises you have made to me for a better future. I pray in the name of Jesus that I will always make you my first priority and live a life that is worthy of your goodness and generosity. Father, in you are all my hopes and my dreams. Amen.

NOTES

_____
_____
_____
_____
_____
_____
_____
_____
_____
_____
_____
_____
_____
_____
_____
_____
_____
_____
_____
_____
_____
_____
_____

NOTES

CHAPTER 19

JOY

*Definition: great delight or happiness caused by something
exceptionally good or satisfying; a source or cause of
keen pleasure or delight*

Well, the cat's surely out of the bag now! The secrets I protected for more than thirty years have been exposed. You know my story, my intimate thoughts and my darkest moments. There is nothing left hidden and not much more to tell. It is ironic that the very thing I feared the most—that my abortions would be discovered—is something I am now exposing to the world.

Some people will wonder why I chose to reveal such personal details of my life. The answer is really pretty simple: it gives me joy to tell people how God brought me out of the pit of despair and changed me. He took the mess I made of my life and transformed it into something worthwhile. He gave me a compassionate heart to help women and men grieving from abortion.

My entire life I built a reputation for focus, hard work, and perseverance. I set big goals, worked hard, and looked for the next challenge. Work and the relationships that were formed through it were the primary sources that I looked to for happiness. Of course, that happiness was temporary and lasted only as long as the task or project did, and then I was back to square one—seeking fulfillment in the next goal and challenge. Basing my happiness on external circumstances kept me on a constant emotional roller coaster. When things were going well, I felt great. When setbacks came, I sunk into self-condemnation and fear. Ironically, that mode of operating served me just fine for a long time and success made me feel proud and accomplished. But it never brought me *joy*.

It was not until I experienced healing from my abortions that I discovered a lasting source of joy that keeps me levelheaded and secure, no matter how high or low my circumstances climb or fall. Things changed when I confronted my past and recognized that abortion is a sin. Admitting my guilt and asking God to forgive me was a big step. An even bigger step was letting go of my guilt and believing he actually did forgive me. This was the beginning of my new relationship with Jesus Christ. No longer dependent on external events or circumstances or my ever-changing relationships, I know that the joy of the Lord is lasting because it is based on God's presence within me.

Yet, it is inevitable that circumstances of life might thrust us backward, shaking our faith in God's goodness and mercy. What happens if you find yourself infertile or experience miscarriage? What if you do all the healing work discussed in this book and your marriage still fails or you never find the love of your life? Since post-abortive women can have a higher incidence of breast cancer, what does it mean if you develop the disease? What if you continue to struggle with anxiety or addiction?

I wrestled with some of those questions myself. Four years after my Rachel's Vineyard experience, my marriage ended and divorce was a devastating blow. It was frightening and lonely to be forty-nine years old, on my own with only a part-time job for support. A year later, I needed major abdominal surgery, and one year later, I developed breast cancer. I worried, "Is God punishing me?"

It is true that there can be far-reaching consequences to abortion, and you cannot earn your way out of them or avoid any discipline God chooses for you. But his discipline is different from punishment because it teaches us to learn from our mistakes rather than making us suffer for them. Setbacks and hardships will almost certainly occur throughout your life. There may or may not be a connection to your abortion. But you can withstand crushing disappointment if you remain faithful and do not allow yourself to loop back into blaming yourself or God—and refuse to give up your joy.

Certainly you may need to grieve for your heartbreak or lost dreams, but refuse to fall back into the trap of self-condemnation. When setbacks occur, call out to God and ask him, "What is your goal for this time in my life?" Rest assured that God *will* answer, and he will daily restore any brokenness you encounter by offering you his promise of a plan and a future so that you might have abundant joy.

Now, I hear some of you thinking, "But I don't *deserve* to be happy. I aborted my own child. He or she doesn't get to be happy, why should I?"

Jerry Sittser, professor and author, asks the question another way after losing his wife, daughter and mother in a horrific car accident, *"Is it possible to feel sorrow for the rest of our lives and yet to find joy at the same time?[20]"* He describes it as a delicate tension—the need to mourn our losses yet go on living.

Through God's mercy, we have been forgiven of our abortion. Through God's grace he is allowing us, actually inviting us, to reconsider our purpose, define new priorities, and go forward in a new direction. Aware of new possibilities and a greater depth of character and faith, we can and we *must* set a new direction for our lives. Sittser writes, *"God's forgiveness will show us that he wants to take our losses and somehow bring them back upon us in the form of a blessing. That is the promise of true transformation; that is the power of the love of God.[21]"*

Rather than allowing your abortion to abort your own life, you too can be transformed and live a joy-filled life. God's grace and mercy come to all of us. But you must be ready to see and willing to receive these gifts. I am a prime example of how God took the mess I made of my life and created something wonderful. You can be too!

REFLECTION EXERCISE

The Joy of the Lord

God has wonderful plans for us and he wants us to experience the best in life. Yet, sometimes circumstances get in the way and our emotions overpower us. We can sink into negativity pretty quickly. According to Dr. Barbara Fredrickson, *"We have a surprising amount of control over the emotions we feel. This is especially true of positive emotions. We can turn them on almost whenever we choose. And, nearly always, we can coax them to linger just a bit longer.*[22]*"*

The following exercise is adapted from Dr. Fredrickson's book, *Positivity*, where she suggests a number of ways to broaden your mind and change your perspective. Review the following tools and choose one or two that you can begin to put into practice.

Tool #1: Create High-Quality Connections

There are all kinds of people, some more positive than others. Make a list of the people you know who seem to have a positive, optimistic outlook on life. Choose one or two of these people and make a commitment to develop an even stronger relationship with them, perhaps by spending more time together, talking on the phone, and fellowshipping together.

Tool #2: Cultivate Kindness

Dr. Fredrickson challenges us to set a goal of performing five new acts of kindness a day. Target actions that make a difference and that take real effort on your part. Such examples can include designating prayer time for a particular person's need or reaching out to a new face in the neighborhood, among many other opportunities presented in our daily lives. Why? Notice the good feelings that come with increasing your kindness and how relationships seem to grow stronger.

Tool #3: Develop Distractions

When negativity gets a grip on you, you need something to break it. The goal is to get your mind off your problem. One thing you can do is recite the calming phrase you developed in the Reflection Exercise in Chapter 10. Another option is to brainstorm a list of ten healthy distractions, coming up with activities you can turn to on the spur-of-the-moment rather than sinking into the pit. Keep this list handy in order to refer to it on a regular basis, and make sure you budget time in your schedule for these spirit-filling actions.

Tool #4: Learn and Apply Your Strengths

What are you really good at doing? If you are not sure, you can take the online assessment referenced in *Positivity,* available at www.authentichappiness.com. Research shows that people who report the greatest degrees of happiness and success are those who regularly use their top strengths. Once you know yours, make a commitment to find ways to use your strengths each day.

Tool #5: Pray

I start off every day by reading my Bible and praying, even if I only have five minutes. Pour your heart out to God and ask him to guide your day and fill you with positive and hopeful thoughts.

Tool #6: Make Gratitude a Habit

Create a "gratitude journal" and develop the practice of writing down the things you are thankful for. Be specific, writing a few sentences to describe what happened and why it is important. Notice if it was an answer to prayer. Developing this practice inspires confidence and hope for even greater blessings to come.

Tool #7: Create Your Personal Vision

This valuable exercise will take some time, but it can be very fulfilling and motivating. Imagine yourself one year from now. What is your best hope for the future? Imagine that everything has gone as well as it possibly could and things turned out even better than you had hoped. Visualize yourself at your best. Write down everything you can remember, describing your surroundings, feelings, and emotions. Do this exercise over several days, and at the end of one week, review what you have written. If your life really turned out this way, would you be happy? If not, revise your vision to make it so. What are some steps you can take today, in the next week, and the next month to fulfill your dream?

Tool #8: Put on the Armor of God

When you find yourself sinking into the trench of negativity, be prepared to substitute God's promises to restore your hope, confidence, and joy. Look up several of following Scriptures and copy them onto index cards. Memorize the verse and repeat it silently or aloud when you are troubled.

Psalm 32:2

Isaiah 61:2

Nehemiah 8:10

Luke 1:58

John 16:24

Romans 12:12

The Joy of the Lord

Discover joy in God's Word:

Praise the Lord!
For he has heard my cry for mercy.
The Lord is my strength and shield.
I trust him with all my heart.
He helps me, and my heart is filled with joy.
I burst out in songs of thanksgiving.
The Lord gives his people strength.
He is a safe fortress for his anointed king.
Psalm 28:6-8 (NLT)

Pray:

Father God, you have taken me on a journey of self discovery that has been difficult and painful. But it has been worth it because I have experienced emotional and spiritual growth. As I came to know myself and my abortion experience better, you replaced my heartbreak, guilt, and shame with your love and faithfulness. In coming to know you, I have finally learned what it really feels like to be joyful and peaceful. There are no words to express how much I love you and want to grow even closer to you. I will do my best to never stop trusting you. Bring people into my life who will strengthen my faith and knowledge of you. Help me to continue to grow as a good and loving person. Use my life and even this painful abortion experience for your glory. Thank you, Father, for everything. Amen.

NOTES

FINAL THOUGHTS

The emotional consequences of abortion are complicated and often misunderstood. Heartbreak, shame, guilt, fear, and other painful emotions make it challenging for a woman to deal with her experience. In the process of accepting my own past moral failures, I have suffered through every one of the difficult emotions I wrote about in this book. Like many, I had an exaggerated sense of responsibility for making things turn out right after my abortions and an underdeveloped sense of humility for believing in my power to do so.

For the longest time, I could not bring myself to ask God for forgiveness. Then I got into the habit of asking for it over and over again because I never *felt* forgiven. Accepting God's forgiveness for my abortions was a significant turning point, but I never would have reached it if I had waited until I *felt* forgiven. Did you notice that there is no chapter in this book about an emotion of forgiveness? That's because forgiveness is *not* a feeling. It is a decision of faith. It is an act of love.

My life began to change when I chose to believe that God loves me so much that he sent his only Son, Jesus Christ, to die for my sins, including my three abortions. His forgiveness is the anchor I cling to every day because it is the only way I can make sense of what has happened in my life and believe that I have a hope and a future.

Many women ask me, "Will I ever get over my abortion?" My answer is, "Yes, but you will never forget it." I am living proof that you can be healed from emotional pain and move on to live a full, joyful life. Of course, I still have times of sadness and regret, but the difference is that those difficult emotions no longer rule my life.

I let God make his way into my life and change me. Through God's strength and the mentors he placed in my life, I found another way to live. You might wonder, "What way do you now live?" I can honestly say I live more meaningfully, more intentionally—but not without God's daily provision through his son's sacrifice on the cross. Jesus is the way into your broken heart and he will heal it. Jesus is the way into your troubled mind and he will restore it. There is no other way but Jesus.

If you would like Jesus to come into your life, you can take a step of faith and commit yourself to Christ by sincerely saying the following prayer:

God, I know that my abortion was a sin and that it has driven a wedge between us. I am truly sorry and regret my abortion. I am leaving my past behind and turning my heart over to you. Please forgive me and help me not to sin again.

I believe that your Son, Jesus Christ, died for my sins, was resurrected from the dead, and is alive and hears my prayer. I invite Jesus to capture my heart and rule in my life from this day forward.

Please send your Holy Spirit to heal my hurts and help me to do your will for the rest of my life. And when I fall, help me to trust you to pick me up and start over again. Thank you for loving me so much! In Jesus' name, I pray. Amen.

Whether you have prayed those words for the first time or you have re-committed yourself to Christ, you can grow closer to him by spending time with God each day. It does not require a long period of time, but developing a consistent daily habit of praying to him and reading his Word will change your life. Ask God to increase your faith and your understanding of his purpose for your life and to reveal how your abortion might be used for a positive result. Find a local church where you can worship God and develop relationships with other followers of Jesus who can answer your questions and support you. God will bless you for every step you take closer to him. Please know that I am praying for you—every day!

ENDNOTES

1   "An Overview of Abortion in the United States." Guttmacher Institute. N.p., Jan 2008. Web. 12 June 2009.

2   "Trends in Abortion in the United States, 1973–2002." N.p., Jan 2003. Web. 30 June 2009.

3   Burke, Theresa. Forbidden Grief. Springfield, IL: Acorn, 2007. 291-304. Print.

4   Burke 120.

5   Burke, Theresa. Forbidden Grief. p. 146.

6   Bradshaw, John (1988). "Bradshaw on: The Family" Health Communications:Deerfield Beach, FL.

7   Meyer, Joyce. Approval Addiction. Nashville, TN: FaithWords, 2005. Print.

8   John Paul II. Evangelium Vitae: On the Value and Inviolability of Human Life.
    Encyclical Letter. Washington: United States Catholic Conference, 1995.

9   Broen AN, Moum T, Bodtker AS, Ekeberg O. The course of mental health after miscarriage and induced abortion: a longitudinal, five-year follow-up study. BMC Med 2005; 3:51.

10 Burke 128.

11 "NIMH Anxiety Disorders." National Institutes of Health. N.p., n.d. Web. 10 Jan 2010.

12 Adapted with permission. Lynn, Adele B. The EQ Difference. New York, NY: AMACOM, 2005.

13 Chisholm, Alan L. "Coping With Envy." Psychotherapy and Spirituality Institute. N.p., n.d. Web. 15 Mar 2010.

14 Wilson, Barbara. The Invisible Bond. Colorado Springs, CO: Multnomah, 2006. 31-32. Print.

15 Keller, Timothy. Sermon recorded at Redeemer Presbyterian Church, New York City,

16 MacArthur, John. Safe in the Arms of God. Nashville, TN: Thomas Nelson, 2003. 61. Print.

17 MacArthur 99.

18 Jones, Laurie Beth. The Path. New York, NY: Hyperion, 1996. Print.

19 May, Gerald G., M.D. Addiction and Grace. San Francisco, CA: Harper, 1988. 18-19. Print.

20 Sittser, Jerry. A Grace Disguised. Grand Rapids, MI: Zondervan. 2004. 50. Print.

21 Sittser 105.

22 Frederickson, Barbara, Ph.D. Positivity. New York, NY: Crown, 2009. 51. Print.

NOTES

NOTES

NOTES

NOTES

Jane Abbate knows about abortion and how it changes a life forever. Through firsthand experience with her own abortions, and through her years of work with women as a Rachel's Vineyard retreat team volunteer and *Forgiven and Set Free* Bible study leader, she has built a solid foundation for helping others deal with their experience of abortion. She lives the healing process she teaches: Face the past, mourn the losses, turn, and draw closer to God.

Jane is the founder of Messy Miracles, a ministry which helps people who struggle with guilt, shame, and regret to recover from the past and lead a fulfilling life. She is a popular speaker who spreads a message of hope and God's forgiveness and love. Jane is a certified professional business coach and makes her home with her husband, Bill, in Pittsburgh, PA.

Jane is available for speaking engagements and can be contacted through her website www.messymiracles.org, by email to jane@messymiracles.org or by writing to:

Jane Abbate

Messy Miracles

PO Box 22, Wildwood, PA 15091-1001

Made in the USA
Charleston, SC
07 November 2013